D0128461

BEAD FANTASIES III
STILL MORE BEAUTIFUL, EASY-TO-MAKE JEWELRY

SAMEJIMA Takako

JAPAN PUBLICATIONS TRADING CO., LTD.

TABLE OF CONTENTS

3   The magic of complementary pieces

36   Beads used for the jewelry in this book

37   Twin gemstone pieces

62   Gemstones

63   Combination patterns

75   Basic techniques

78   Useful tools

READ THIS BEFORE YOU BEGIN A PROJECT.

◆ If your vendor doesn't carry the designer or gemstone beads specified in this book, feel free to substitute beads of the same size and shape.

◆ In our list of supplies for each project, we sometimes specify the manufacturers of a particular type of bead. T stands for Toho, M for Miyuki and H for Hiroshima. Gemstone beads, being natural objects, vary in size. Sizes given in this book are meant to serve as guidelines.

◆ We include approximate lengths for nylon thread and wire. Since the holes in gemstone beads are traditionally very small, we recommend using thin (0.205mm diameter) nylon thread.

◆ In the drawings, we indicate the starting point with a ★ symbol, and the ending point with a ☽ symbol.

Translated by Connie Prener

©2006 English tex., Japan Publications Trading Co., Ltd.
English edition by Japan Publications Trading Co.Ltd. 1-2-1, Sarugaku-cho, Chiyoda-ku, Tokyo 101-0064, Japan.

Original Japanese edition published by Nihon Bungei-sha Co., Ltd., 1-7 Kanda Jinbo-cho, Chiyoda-ku, Tokyo 101-8407, Japan.

First edition, First printing : March 2006

Distributors:
United States: Kodansha America, Inc. through Oxford University Press, 198 Madison Avenue, New York, NY 10016.
Canada: Fitzhenry & White Side Ltd., 195 All States Parkway, Ontario, L3R 4T8.
Australia and New Zealand: Bookwise International Pty Ltd. 174 Cormack Road, Wingfield, SA 5013, Australia.
Asia and other countries: Japan Publications Trading Co., Ltd., 1-2-1, Sarugaku-cho, Chiyoda-ku, Tokyo 101-0064, Japan.

ISBN-13: 978-4-88996-198-0
ISBN-10: 4-88996-198-4

Printed in Japan

THE MAGIC OF COMPLEMENTARY PIECES

By pairing one piece of jewelry with another, complementary or coordinating piece (one that differs in color or design — a ring and a necklace, or a necklace and earrings, for instance), we can create an effect that is fresher and livelier than the one you get from matched pieces. The coordinating items in this book can, of course, be worn by themselves, but we hope you'll try mixing and matching them, too.

Citrus Ring p.7

Marmalade Necklace p.6

Coordinates: Group 1

Marmalade Necklace & Citrus Ring

We combined a motif featuring fire opal beads with fine chain to create an elegant, sophisticated necklace. The motif's raspberry shape makes the coordinating ring unique. The metal beads peeking out from the ring harmonize with the necklace.

MARMALADE NECKLACE

Supplies

10 6 x 8-mm teardrop fire opal beads

6 3-mm carnelian beads

2 4-mm red agate beads

Round white freshwater pearl beads (5 3-mm beads, 2 4-mm beads and 1 6-mm bead)

15 1-mm seed beads (matte gold: M182)

13-mm (diameter) perforated finding

2 26-cm lengths chain

10 2-cm headpins

4 3-mm jump rings

Spring clasp

Adjustable chain closure

2 60-cm lengths nylon thread

1

Make motif, beginning by stringing beads on center of nylon thread.

3 seed beads

Fire opal bead

★

2

String more beads. Pass thread through a fire opal bead strung in Step

3-mm freshwater pearl bead

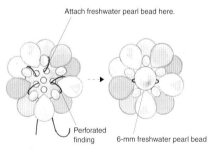

3

Attach motif to perforated finding with a new length of thread. Attach 6-mm freshwater pearl bead to center of finding.

Attach freshwater pearl bead here.

Perforated finding

6-mm freshwater pearl bead

4

Join halves of perforated finding (see p. 76 for instructions).

Cut tabs in half.

Bottom half of finding

5

Attach motif and Components a-e to chain. Attach clasp to one end and adjustable chain closure to other with jump rings.

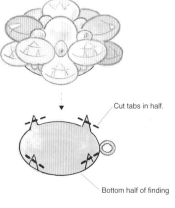

Adjustable chain closure

Spring clasp

Jump rings

26cm chain

Components

a.

Headpin

Carnelian bead

(Make 6.)

b.

Red agate bead

(Make 2.)

c.

4-mm freshwater pearl bead

(Make 2.)

a   a

c   c

a   a

b   b

a   a

Jump rings

CITRUS RING

Supplies

20 4 x 6-mm teardrop olive quartz glass beads
11 2-mm metal beads (bronze)
51 2-mm seed beads (green: M 307)

2 60-cm lengths nylon thread

1

Make motif, beginning by stringing beads on center of nylon thread.

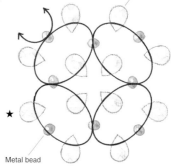

Olive quartz bead

Metal bead

2

Add beads, picking up metal beads strung in Step 1 as you go along.

Metal bead

Set this end aside.

Olive quartz bead

Form an intersection in a metal bead.

3

String new beads on one end of thread. Work around motif, then tie thread to thread set aside earlier.

Olive quartz bead

Pull threads to form dome.

4

Weave band, beginning and ending by picking up an olive quartz bead on motif. Tie threads and finish off.

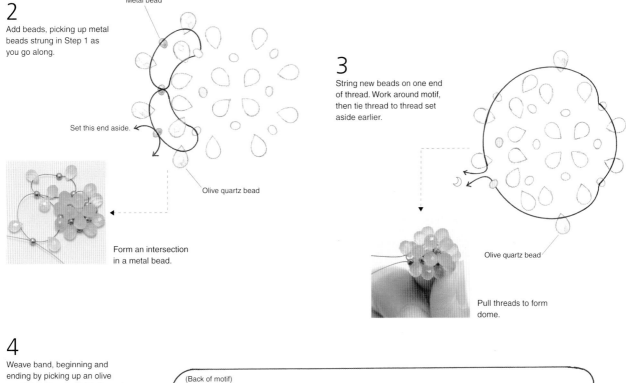

(Back of motif)

1 2 3 4 5 6 7 8 9 10   13 14

Seed bead

GRASS-GREEN NECKLACE & MIMOSA RING

Grass-Green
Necklace   p.10

Mimosa Ring   p.11

Coordinates: Group 2

GRASS-GREEN NECKLACE & MIMOSA RING

These coordinates combine the colors of Nature: grass green, yellow and white. The colors are subdued, but the necklace and the ring's motif add luxurious volume. Only in natural stones do we find the lustrous green of the grossular garnet and peridot beads.

Variation: **Earrings**

The necklace motif, with its elegant freshwater-pearl center, is perfect for earrings.

Variation: Earrings   p.11

09

GRASS-GREEN NECKLACE & EARRINGS

Supplies (Necklace)

45 6 x 8-mm teardrop grossular garnet beads
7 4.5-mm round freshwater pearl beads (white)
8 4-mm Swarovski bicone crystal beads (light Colorado topaz)
6 4-mm round fire-polished beads
169 2-mm 3-cut beads (green/gold: T CR513)

2 crimp beads
3-mm jump ring
13-mm (diameter) perforated finding
Spring clasp
Adjustable chain closure
2 60-cm lengths nylon thread
70cm nylon-coated wire

1

Make motif, beginning by stringing beads on center of nylon thread.

Form intersections in 3-cut beads.

Grossular garnet bead

3-cut bead

2

Add more beads, picking up 3-cut beads as you go along. Tie threads and finish off.

Grossular garnet bead

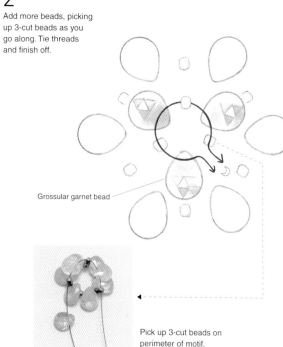

Pick up 3-cut beads on perimeter of motif.

3

Attach motif and freshwater pearl bead to perforated finding.

Freshwater pearl bead

Attach motif to finding here.

Perforated finding

4

Once motif has been secured, join two halves of finding (see directions on p. 76).

Cut tabs in half.

Jump ring

Bottom of finding

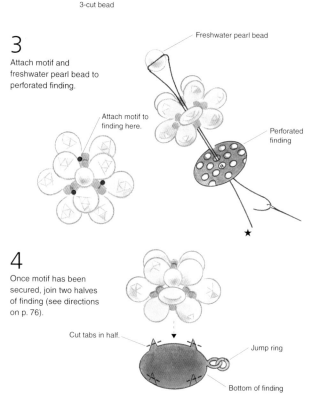

5

String beads on nylon-coated wire. Add a crimp bead at each end of necklace. Attach clasp to one end and adjustable chain closure to other.

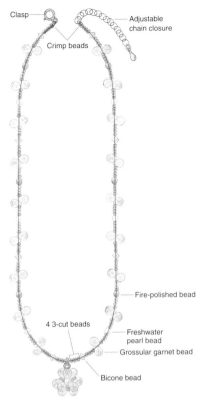

Clasp

Adjustable chain closure

Crimp beads

Fire-polished bead

4 3-cut beads

Freshwater pearl bead

Grossular garnet bead

Bicone bead

Supplies (Earrings)

18 6 x 8-mm teardrop grossular garnet beads
2 4.5-mm round freshwater pearl beads (white)
18 2-mm 3-cut beads (green/gold: T CR513)

13-mm (diameter) perforated post earring findings
4 60-cm lengths nylon thread

Make two motifs, following Steps 1-3 of instructions for necklace. Attach motifs to earring finding (see directions on p. 76).

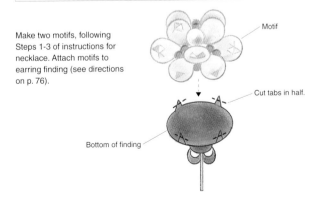

Motif

Cut tabs in half.

Bottom of finding

MIMOSA RING

Supplies

6 x 7.5-mm oval moonstone bead
6 x 8-mm oval cubic zirconia (citrine)
4 3.5 x 4.5-mm button peridot beads
2 3 x 4.5-mm button citrine beads
4 chip mother-of-pearl beads (white)
Round freshwater pearl beads
(2 3-mm white beads, 2 5-mm green beads)
2 4-mm Swarovski bicone crystal beads (light Colorado topaz)
10 3-mm seed beads (matte gold: M 182)
44 2-mm seed beads (matte gold: M 182)

80cm nylon thread

1

String beads on center of nylon thread. Form an intersection in first 3-mm seed bead strung.

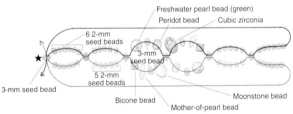

Freshwater pearl bead (green)
Peridot bead
Cubic zirconia
6 2-mm seed beads
3-mm seed bead
5 2-mm seed beads
3-mm seed bead
Bicone bead
Moonstone bead
Mother-of-pearl bead

2

Add more beads, picking up beads from foundation row as you go along. Tie threads together and finish off.

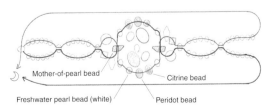

Mother-of-pearl bead
Citrine bead
Freshwater pearl bead (white)
Peridot bead

MERCURY NECKLACE & CHERRY BLOSSOM RING

The necklace, with its cool pale blue and green gemstone beads,
is an ideal partner of the ring, with its bead-cluster cherry
blossoms. The silver beads add sparkle to the necklace, and
crystal bicone beads add brilliance to the ring.

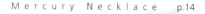

Mercury Necklace   p.14

Cherry Blossom Ring   p.15

Variation: **Ring**

Green beads replace the pink
colors of the cherry blossom
ring for a more subdued look.

Variation: Ring   p.15

Coordinates: Group 3

MERCURY
NECKLACE &
CHERRY
BLOSSOM
RING

MERCURY NECKLACE

Supplies

Amazonite beads (8 6-mm beads, 1 10-mm bead)
Round chrysoprase beads (4 3-mm beads, 32 4-mm beads)
Round green aventurine beads (26 3-mm beads, 4 4-mm beads)
14 round 4-mm freshwater pearl beads (white)
154 2-mm seed beads (silver: M 181)
20 1-mm seed beads (silver: M 181)

2 crimp beads
Spring clasp
Adjustable chain closure
80cm nylon thread
60cm nylon-coated wire

1

Make motif, beginning
by stringing beads on
center of nylon
thread.

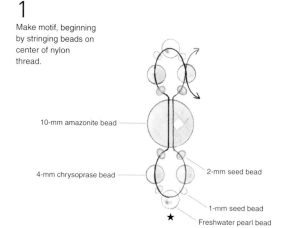

10-mm amazonite bead

4-mm chrysoprase bead

2-mm seed bead

1-mm seed bead

Freshwater pearl bead

★

2

Close circle and set
one end of thread
aside.

Set aside thread
used to string
chrysoprase bead.

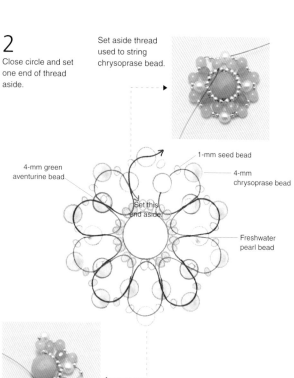

4-mm green
aventurine bead

1-mm seed bead

4-mm
chrysoprase bead

Set this
end aside.

Freshwater
pearl bead

Close circle by passing
thread through freshwater
pearl bead at starting point.

3

After you've worked
around perimeter of
motif, tie thread to
thread end set aside
earlier.

Add beads, picking
up 4-mm
chrysoprase beads
as you go along.

3-mm green
aventurine bead

3-mm
chrysoprase bead

14

4

With nylon-coated wire, pick up beads from motif and string more beads to make necklace. Add a crimp bead at each end of necklace. Attach clasp to one end and adjustable chain closure to other.

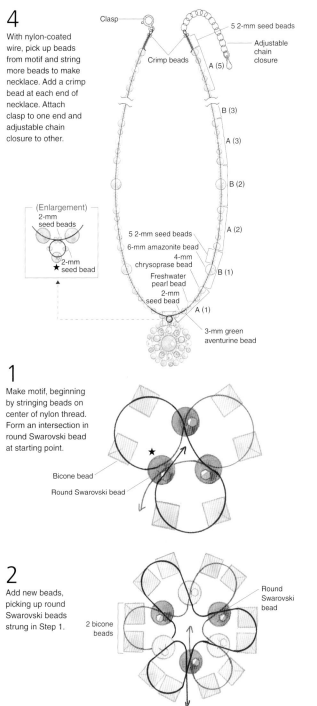

Clasp

5 2-mm seed beads

Adjustable chain closure

Crimp beads

A (5)

B (3)

A (3)

B (2)

A (2)

5 2-mm seed beads

6-mm amazonite bead

4-mm chrysoprase bead

Freshwater pearl bead

2-mm seed bead

B (1)

A (1)

3-mm green aventurine bead

(Enlargement)

2-mm seed beads

2-mm seed bead

★

CHERRY RING

Supplies

(Purple ring)

48 3-mm Swarovski bicone crystal beads (violet opal)

12 3-mm Swarovski round crystal beads (fuchsia)

21 3-mm round fire-polished beads (light sapphire CAL)

42 2-mm seed beads (pale blue: T 176)

2 3-mm seed beads (pink: T 332)

3 60-cm lengths nylon thread

(Green ring)

48 3-mm Swarovski bicone crystal beads (Pacific opal)

12 3-mm Swarovski round crystal beads (peridot satin)

21 3-mm fire-polished beads (light topaz CAL)

42 2-mm seed beads (yellow: M 234)

2 3-mm seed beads (green: T 940)

3 60-cm lengths nylon thread

1

Make motif, beginning by stringing beads on center of nylon thread. Form an intersection in round Swarovski bead at starting point.

Bicone bead

Round Swarovski bead

2

Add new beads, picking up round Swarovski beads strung in Step 1.

2 bicone beads

Round Swarovski bead

3

Add new beads, picking up round Swarovski beads strung in Step 2. Add 3-mm seed beads, then tie threads and finish off. Make 2 of these motifs.

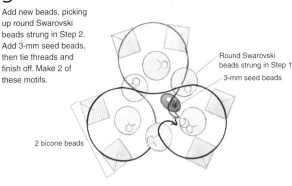

Round Swarovski beads strung in Step 1

3-mm seed beads

2 bicone beads

4

With new length of nylon thread, pick up 3-mm seed bead from motif. Weave band. Tie threads and finish off.

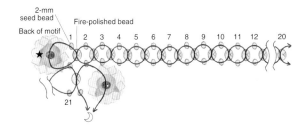

2-mm seed bead

Fire-polished bead

Back of motif

1 2 3 4 5 6 7 8 9 10 11 12 20

21

Coordinates: Group 4

SPANGLE
NECKLACE &
MULTI
COLORED
RING

Multicolored Ring   p.19

Coordinates: Group 4

SPANGLE NECKLACE & MULTICOLORED RING

Jet black onyx lends an air of mystery to this necklace, even when combined with other colors. The sequins woven into the all-black motif keep it from being too serious. Together, the necklace and the multicolored ring form a perfect union.

Spangle Necklace   p.18

Variation: Ring   p.19

Variation: Ring

We used the necklace motif to make a ring. The thin band accentuates the delicate motif.

SPANGLE NECKLACE & RING

Supplies (Necklace)

12 4-mm round onyx beads

7-mm Swarovski round crystal bead (jet)

24 3-mm Swarovski bicone crystal beads (jet)

14 5-mm round fire-polished beads (jet AB)

208 2-mm seed beads (black: M 401)

8 4-mm sequins (black)

8 5-mm sequins (black)

2 crimp beads

Spring clasp

Adjustable chain closure

80cm nylon thread

60cm nylon-coated wire

1

Make motif, beginning by stringing beads on center of nylon thread.

Form an intersection in a bicone bead,

3 seed beads

4-mm sequin

Seed bead

5-mm sequin

Bicone bead

Fire-polished bead

★

2

Add more beads, picking up fire-polished beads on perimeter as you go along. Pass threads through beads at center, tie together and finish off.

Add seed beads and onyx beads.

Seed bead

Onyx bead

Round Swarovski bead

3

Pass nylon-coated wire through onyx bead on motif. Add beads to make necklace. Add a crimp bead at each end of necklace. Attach clasp to one end and adjustable chain closure to other.

Clasp

Adjustable chain closure

Crimp beads

5

4

3

2

Bicone bead

Seed bead

8 seed beads

Fire-polished bead

8 seed beads

Onyx bead

1

Supplies (Ring)

4 4-mm round onyx beads

10 3-mm Swarovski bicone crystal beads (jet)

7-mm Swarovski round crystal bead (jet)

4 5-mm round fire-polished beads (jet AB)

55 2-mm seed beads (black: M401)

8 4-mm sequins (black)

8 5-mm sequins (black)

Nylon thread (1 60-cm length, 1 80-cm length)

Make motif, following Steps 1 and 2 of directions for necklace. With 60cm nylon thread, pick up an onyx bead on motif and make band. Tie threads together and finish off.

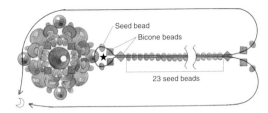

MULTICOLORED RING

Supplies

6 4-mm round garnet beads

6 4-mm round gold sandstone beads

6 4-mm round turquoise beads

6 4-mm round freshwater pearl beads (light gray)

4-mm round glass beads (6 pink, 6 green)

6 2-mm metal beads (gold)

84 2-mm 3-cut beads (bronze: T CR221)

1m nylon thread

1

Begin stringing beads at center of nylon thread. Form intersections in metal bead and 2 3-cut beads.

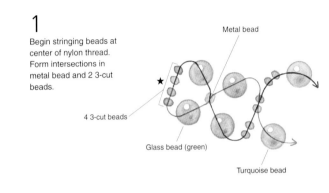

2

After you've added the gold sandstone beads, form an intersection in 3-cut beads at starting point.

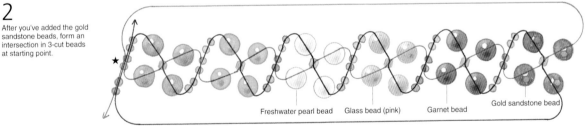

3

Make outside edge, picking up 3-cut beads. Tie threads and finish off.

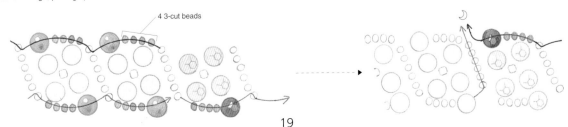

SILVER
NECKLACE &
CROSS RING

Cross Ring   p.23

Silver Necklace   p.22

Coordinates: Group 5

SILVER NECKLACE & CROSS RING

The mother-of-pearl and silver bead combination and the small, simple motif add up to a necklace you can wear for any occasion. We chose a monochrome design for the ring, with a cross accent at the center.

Variation: Ring   p.22

Variation: Ring

We used the necklace motif to make this silver ring, which designer beads give a very contemporary look. Wear it with the matching necklace.

SILVER NECKLACE & RING

Supplies (Necklace)

6-mm round mother-of-pearl bead (white)
Round silver beads (6 3-mm beads, 2-4-mm beads)
Silver designer beads (6 3 x 5-mm beads, 1 3.6 x 7.7-mm bead)
190 2-mm round metal beads (silver)

2 crimp beads
Spring clasp
Adjustable chain closure
60cm nylon thread
60cm nylon-coated wire

Supplies (Ring)

6-mm round mother-of-pearl bead (white)
6 3-mm round silver beads
6 3 x 5-mm silver designer beads
44 2-mm metal beads (silver)
2 60-cm lengths nylon thread

1

String beads on nylon thread, following directions in Step 1 of instructions for necklace motif. Tie threads together and finish off.

Mother-of-pearl bead

Silver designer bead

Round silver bead

★

2

With new thread, pick up beads from motif and make band. Tie threads together and finish off.

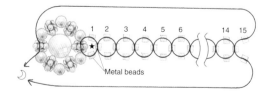

Metal beads

1

Make motif, beginning by stringing beads on center of nylon thread. Tie threads together and finish off.

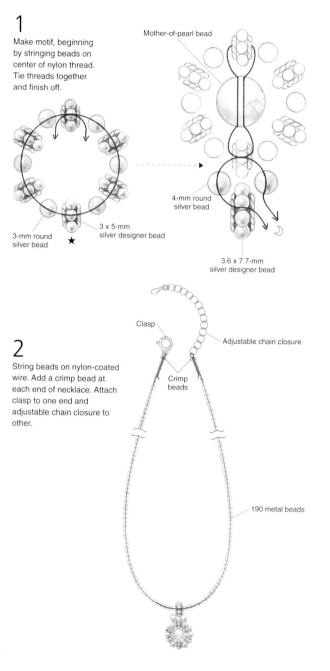

Mother-of-pearl bead

3-mm round silver bead

3 x 5-mm silver designer bead

★

4-mm round silver bead

3.6 x 7.7-mm silver designer bead

2

String beads on nylon-coated wire. Add a crimp bead at each end of necklace. Attach clasp to one end and adjustable chain closure to other.

Clasp

Crimp beads

Adjustable chain closure

190 metal beads

CROSS RING

Supplies

White ring

60 2-mm round howlite beads

4 6-mm Swarovski button crystal beads (white alabaster)

72 1-mm seed beads (white: T 122)

7-mm (diameter) cross (silver)

2 80-cm lengths nylon thread

Black ring

60 2-mm round onyx beads

4 6-mm Swarovski button crystal beads (jet)

72 1-mm seed beads (black: M 401)

7-mm (diameter) cross (silver)

2 80-cm lengths nylon thread

1

Make motif, beginning by stringing beads on center of nylon thread.

Silver cross

Seed beads

Howlite beads

Button beads

★

2

Add seed beads, picking up button beads on perimeter. Set one end of thread aside.

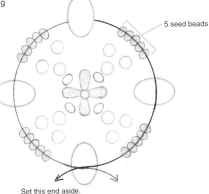

5 seed beads

Set this end aside.

3

String 5 howlite beads at a time on to other end of thread, working your way around motif. Pass thread through seed beads and button beads. Tie thread to thread end set aside earlier.

5 howlite beads

4

With new thread, pick up a button bead from motif and make band. Tie threads together and finish off.

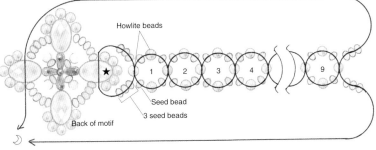

Howlite beads

Seed bead

3 seed beads

Back of motif

23

Comet Necklace   p.26

Onyx Ring   p.27

Variation:
Ring   p.27

Coordinates: Group 6

COMET NECKLACE &
ONYX RING

These pieces feature an Italian-style motif, with curves and a three-dimensional structure. The onyx beads forming the edging on the motif, and gracing the necklace, add richness. The luxurious onyx ring makes the perfect partner for the necklace.

Variation: **Ring**

We rearranged the turquoise, coral and freshwater pearl beads for this ring. With its matte texture, this piece pays homage to the 1960s.

Variation:
Brooch   p.27

Variation: **Brooch**

This three-dimensional motif makes a marvelous brooch. We added a larger turquoise bead at the center.

24

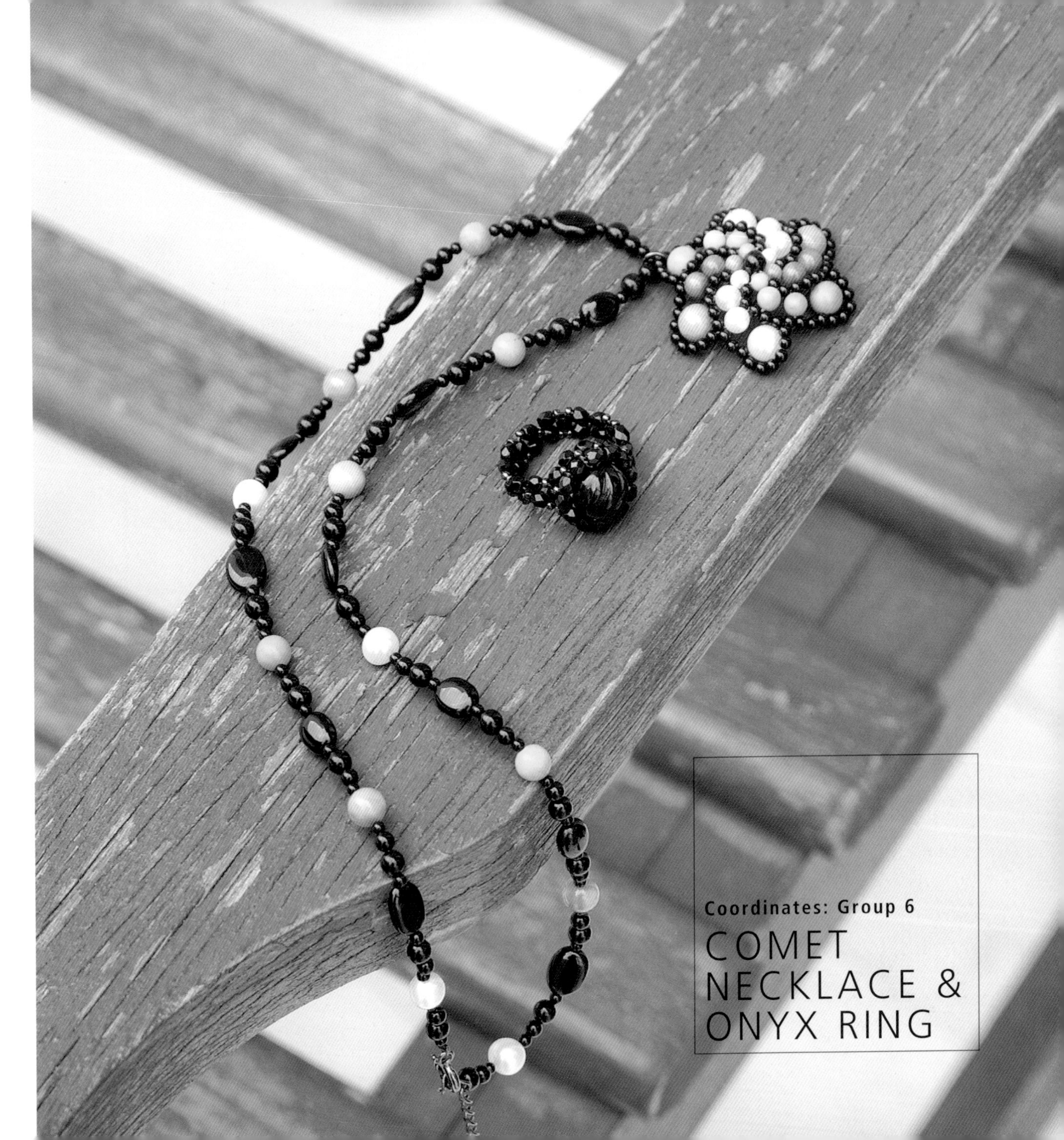

Coordinates: Group 6

COMET NECKLACE & ONYX RING

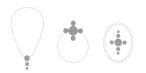

COMET NECKLACE, RING & BROOCH

Supplies (Necklace)

12 6 x 8-mm oval onyx beads
Round onyx beads (142 2-mm, 26 3-mm, 27 4-mm beads)
Round turquoise beads (2 3-mm, 4 4-mm, 6 6-mm beads)
Round coral beads (2 3-mm, 4 4-mm, 6 6-mm beads)
Round freshwater pearl beads (white) (2 3-mm, 4 4-mm, 6 6-mm beads)

2 crimp beads
6-mm jump ring
Spring clasp
Adjustable chain closure
Nylon thread (1 20-cm length, 1 90-cm length)
70cm nylon-coated wire

1

Make motif, beginning by stringing beads 25cm from one end of 90cm nylon thread.

Set aside (short end).
4-mm turquoise bead
3-mm turquoise bead
4-mm coral bead
3-mm coral bead
3-mm freshwater pearl bead
4-mm freshwater pearl bead
2-mm onyx bead

2

Working around perimeter with one end of thread, add more beads. Tie thread to end set aside earlier and finish off.

4-mm turquoise bead
4-mm coral bead
4-mm freshwater pearl bead
3 2-mm onyx beads
6-mm turquoise bead
6-mm freshwater pearl bead
6-mm coral bead
6 2-mm onyx beads

Add more beads, picking up 3 onyx beads at a time.

3

Make center of motif, using 20cm nylon thread.

4-mm onyx bead

4

Attach a jump ring to motif. Pass nylon-coated wire through jump ring, and make necklace. Add a crimp bead at each end of necklace. Attach clasp to one end and adjustable chain closure to other.

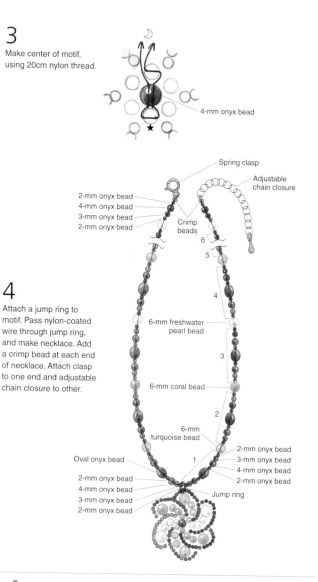

Spring clasp
2-mm onyx bead
4-mm onyx bead
3-mm onyx bead
2-mm onyx bead
Crimp beads
Adjustable chain closure
6
5
4
6-mm freshwater pearl bead
3
6-mm coral bead
2
6-mm turquoise bead
Oval onyx bead
2-mm onyx bead
4-mm onyx bead
3-mm onyx bead
2-mm onyx bead
1
2-mm onyx bead
3-mm onyx bead
4-mm onyx bead
2-mm onyx bead
Jump ring

ONYX RING

Supplies

10-mm round onyx bead
48 3-mm round fire-polished beads (jet)
37 1-mm seed beads (black: M 451)

2 60-cm lengths nylon thread

26

79 2-mm round onyx beads
Round turquoise beads (2 3-mm, 4 4-mm beads, 1 8-mm bead)
Round coral beads (2 3-mm, 4 4-mm beads)
Freshwater pearl beads (white) (2 3-mm, 4 4-mm beads)

Nylon thread (1 20-cm length, 2 70-cm lengths)

54 2-mm round onyx beads
Round turquoise beads (2 3-mm, 4 4-mm, 2 6-mm beads, 1 8-mm bead)
Round coral beads (2 3-mm beads, 4 4-mm, 2 6-mm beads)
Round freshwater pearl beads (white) (2 3-mm, 4 4-mm, 2 6-mm beads)
20-mm perforated brooch back

Nylon thread (1 each 20-cm length, 40-cm length, 80-cm length)

1

Begin stringing beads 25cm from end of 70cm nylon thread.
Tie thread to thread end set aside earlier.

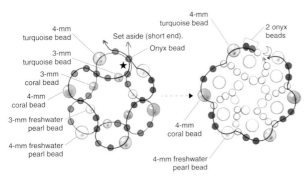

2

Using Step 3 of instructions for necklace as a guide, make center of motif, placing an 8-mm turquoise bead at center. With new length of nylon thread, pick up coral bead on motif and weave band. Tie threads together and finish off.

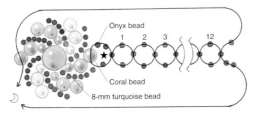

1

String beads on 80cm nylon thread 25cm away from one end.

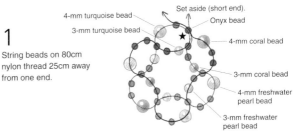

2

Work around perimeter of motif, then tie thread to thread end set aside earlier.

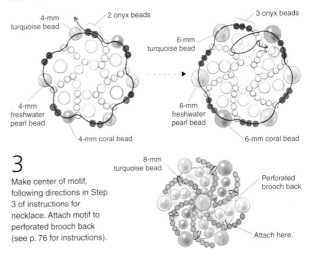

3

Make center of motif, following directions in Step 3 of instructions for necklace. Attach motif to perforated brooch back (see p. 76 for instructions).

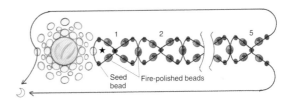

1

Make motif, beginning by stringing beads on center of nylon thread.

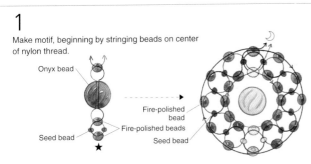

2

Using new thread, pick up a fire-polished bead on motif and weave band. Tie threads together and finish off.

LEAF
NECKLACE &
MOONSTONE
RING

Moonstone Ring   p.30

Leaf Necklace   p.30

Coordinates: Group 7

LEAF NECKLACE &
MOONSTONE RING

The three-strand necklace features leaf-shaped opal beads, with intertwined silver beads and ball chain for a touch of elegance.
The moonstone ring is special because we incorporated ball chain for a subtle effect.

LEAF NECKLACE

Supplies

12 x 18-mm leaf-shaped opal beads (2 blue, 3 pink)
14 6 x 8-mm teardrop labradorite beads
10 4.5 x 6-mm oval rainbow moonstone beads
10 7 x 9-mm teardrop aquamarine beads
14 4-mm round freshwater pearl beads (white)
2-mm seed beads (10 matte pink gold: T 551, 10 green: T 560)
300 2-mm 3-cut beads (silver: M 181)

4 crimp beads
4 3-mm jump rings
2 side-clamp bead tips
50-cm length 1.5-mm (diameter) ball chain
Spring clasp
Adjustable chain closure
2 60-cm lengths nylon-coated wire

1

String a crimp bead on both lengths of nylon-coated wire, 25cm from one end. Compress crimp beads.

Nylon-coated wire

Crimp bead

2

String beads on wire.

Aquamarine bead
Labradorite bead
Freshwater pearl bead
Seed bead (green)
Moonstone bead
Seed bead (matte pink gold)
Leaf bead (pink)
Leaf bead (blue)

MOONSTONE RING

Supplies

34 3.5-mm round moonstone beads
34 3-mm round freshwater pearl beads (white)
34 1-mm seed beads (white: T 122)

7cm 1.5-mm (diameter) ball chain
Nylon thread (2 30-cm lengths, 1 100-cm length)

1

Tie 100cm nylon thread to end of chain at center of thread, as shown in drawing. String beads on thread, forming intersections that enclose chain.

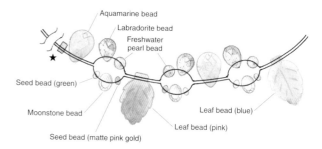

Freshwater pearl bead

Chain

Knot

Moonstone bead

3

String a crimp bead on wire and compress. String beads for necklace, then attach a crimp bead to each end. Attach clasp to one end of necklace and adjustable chain closure to other.

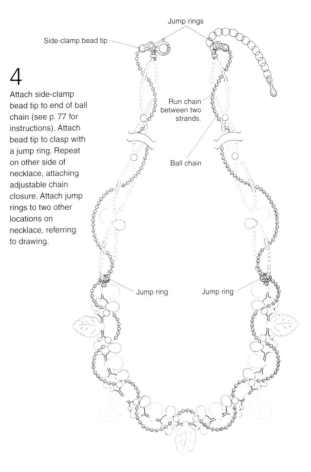

Crimp beads

Clasp

Adjustable chain closure

15 3-cut beads

2

Freshwater pearl bead

Aquamarine bead

Labradorite bead

15 3-cut beads

1

Crimp bead

4

Attach side-clamp bead tip to end of ball chain (see p. 77 for instructions). Attach bead tip to clasp with a jump ring. Repeat on other side of necklace, attaching adjustable chain closure. Attach jump rings to two other locations on necklace, referring to drawing.

Jump rings

Side-clamp bead tip

Run chain between two strands.

Ball chain

Jump ring

Jump ring

2

Repeat Step 1, then close circle by passing thread through beads at starting point. Tie threads together and finish off.

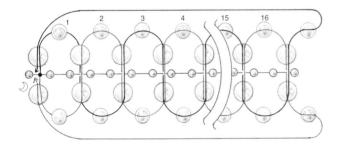

3

With new thread, work around outside edge of ring, picking up freshwater pearl beads and adding seed beads as you go along. Tie threads together and finish off.

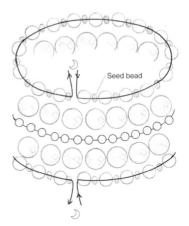

Seed bead

SAPPHIRE
NECKLACE &
STAR
EARRINGS

SAPPHIRE NECKLACE & STAR EARRINGS

The main features of this necklace are the dangling sapphire beads. Coil (or French wire) is interspersed with small carnelian, amethyst and other gemstone beads in rainbow colors. The amethyst beads in the earrings harmonize with the amethyst beads in the necklace.

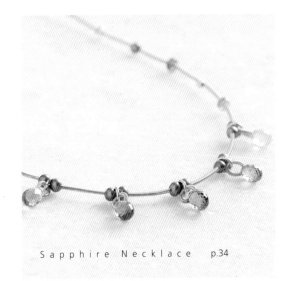

Sapphire Necklace   p.34

Star Earrings   p.34

Heart Earrings   p.35

Variation: Heart Earrings

These earrings feature apatite bead fringe atop heart-shaped blue quartz beads.

Ruby Earrings   p.35

Variation: Ruby Earrings

The pale green prehnite beads combine with tiny rubies to create the illusion of berries on a tiny branch. Another, unique aspect is the diagonally bent wire.

Drop Earrings   p.35

Variation: Drop Earrings

These sweet little earrings have three heart-shaped beads mounted on a teardrop blue quartz bead. The heart beads are gold-plated silver.

SAPPHIRE NECKLACE

Supplies

- 5 4 x 5-mm teardrop sapphire beads (5 different colors)
- 2 3-mm button carnelian beads
- 2 3-mm button amethyst beads
- 2 3-mm button blue quartz beads
- 2 3-mm button peridot beads
- 2 3-mm button citrine beads
- 16 3-mm round freshwater pearl beads (brown)
- 8 2-mm round metal beads (gold)
- 37 1-cm lengths 0.6mm (inner diameter) coil or French wire (gold)
- 2 crimp beads
- 5 4-mm jump rings
- Clasp set
- 5 20-cm lengths nylon thread
- 60cm nylon-coated wire

1

Make components. String coil and sapphire bead on nylon thread. Form a circle and tie thread. Make 5 of these.

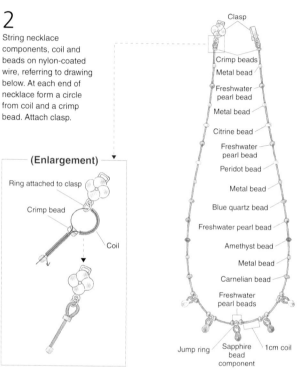

20cm nylon thread — Coil — Sapphire bead

2

String necklace components, coil and beads on nylon-coated wire, referring to drawing below. At each end of necklace form a circle from coil and a crimp bead. Attach clasp.

(Enlargement)

Ring attached to clasp
Crimp bead
Coil

Clasp
Crimp beads
Metal bead
Freshwater pearl bead
Metal bead
Citrine bead
Freshwater pearl bead
Peridot bead
Metal bead
Blue quartz bead
Freshwater pearl bead
Amethyst bead
Metal bead
Carnelian bead
Freshwater pearl beads

Jump ring — Sapphire bead component — 1cm coil

STAR EARRINGS

Supplies

- 2 7-mm star-shaped amethyst beads
- 2 3-mm button carnelian beads
- 2 3-mm button peridot beads
- 2 3-mm mirror ball beads
- Ear wires
- 8 20-cm lengths Artistic Wire (silver)

1

String a star-shaped amethyst bead on wire. Form a circle with wire. Twist as shown in drawing.

Form a circle and wrap wire around base.

Amethyst bead

2

Pass a new length of wire through first circle and twist to form another circle. Cut one end of wire with wire-cutters.

3

Add a carnelian bead. Round wire with round-nose pliers. Wind wire around base of circle several times.

Wind wire here.

Carnelian bead

4

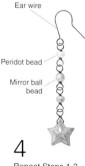

Ear wire
Peridot bead
Mirror ball bead

Repeat Steps 1-3. Attach ear wires.

H E A R T
E A R R I N G S

Supplies

- 2 10-mm heart-shaped blue quartz beads
- 20 3-mm button apatite beads
- 20 5-cm headpins with rounded ends (silver)
- Ear wires (silver)

1

Make 18 of component shown below.

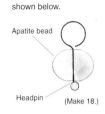

Apatite bead

Headpin   (Make 18.)

2

String heart-shaped blue quartz bead and 9 components on a headpin. Attach ear wire.

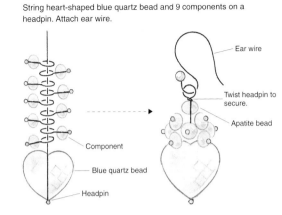

Ear wire

Twist headpin to secure.

Apatite bead

Component

Blue quartz bead

Headpin

R U B Y
E A R R I N G S

Supplies

- 2 5.5 x 9-mm teardrop prehnite beads
- 2 3-mm round freshwater pearl beads (white)
- 2 3 x 4-mm button ruby beads
- 2 3-mm round coral beads

- Ear wires
- 2 30-cm lengths Artistic Wire (gold)

1

Pass wire through prehnite bead and twist for 3mm.

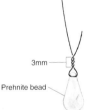

3mm

Prehnite bead

2

Pass one end of wire through coral bead, then twist wire again.

Ear wire

Ruby bead

Freshwater pearl bead

Twist wire.

Coral bead

3

Add freshwater pearl and ruby beads. Attach ear wire.

D R O P
E A R R I N G S

Supplies

- 2 5.5 x 9-mm teardrop blue quartz beads
- 6 4-mm heart-shaped silver beads

- 8 1.5-mm crimp beads
- Ear wires
- 4 20-cm lengths Artistic Wire (silver)

1

Attach wire to blue quartz bead.

Form a circle and wrapwire around base.

Blue quartz bead

2

Attach a new length of wire. String beads. Attach ear wire.

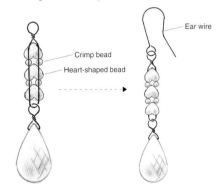

Ear wire

Crimp bead

Heart-shaped bead

Beads Used To Make the Jewelry in This Book

Here we introduce beads commonly used to make jewelry, including those used to make the jewelry in this book. Each type has distinguishing characteristics, for instance, the brilliance of Swarovski crystal beads and glass beads, or the luster of silver beads. Beads come in a wide range of shapes, sizes and materials.

Seed beads

This name applies to all beads cut from long, narrow glass cylinders.

1. 2-mm seed beads
This is probably the most common size of seed bead.

2. 3-mm seed beads

3. 1-mm seed beads

4. 3-cut beads
These beads, which have irregular cuts on their surfaces, typically measure 2mm in diameter.

5. 1-mm 3-cut beads

6. Bugle beads
These are long, narrow beads. The beads in the photograph measure 6mm in length.

Faceted glass beads

These beads have multiple cut surfaces that sparkle in the light. They are made in a variety of ways and are available in many shapes.

7. Fire-polished beads
The surfaces of these beads are melted and then polished to make them glossy.

8. Button-shaped fire-polished beads

9. Round faceted-glass beads
Nearly round beads made by Swarovski.

10. Button-shaped faceted-glass beads
Also made by Swarovski.

11. Bicone crystal beads
Perhaps the best known beads in the Swarovski line.

Other types of beads

The special features of these beads (shape, material, etc.) make them ideal for use as accent beads.

12. Round glass beads
These have smooth, lustrous surfaces.

13. Cat's-eye beads
These have a streak on them that resembles a cat's eye.

14. Coil or French wire
Wound fine wire, cut into short lengths for use in jewelry-making.

15. Metal beads
Most of these are gold- or silver-plated.

16. Silver beads
These sterling silver beads come in a variety of shapes. Some are gold-plated.

Swarovski crystal beads

The Austrian firm Swarovski has been cutting crystals since 1895. The company is famous for its beautiful, high-quality products.

TWIN GEMSTONE PIECES

We designed groupings of jewelry that use the same gemstones, but are different in style.
The lure of gemstones is their adaptability.

Rose Quartz

FRINGED NECKLACE & EARRINGS

Rose quartz combines with silver designer beads for a very sophisticated look.
By using subdued colors, we created fringed pieces that aren't the least bit gaudy.

A symbol of the Greek goddess Aphrodite, rose quartz is said to
encourage the flow of love. The gemstone is also believed to
inspire honesty and gentleness, and to heal broken hearts.

Pink and White Necklace & Ring

These romantic pieces feature, besides rose quartz beads, soft pink coral and freshwater pearl beads.
The necklace has lovely picot details that enhance its beauty.

FRINGED NECKLACE & EARRINGS

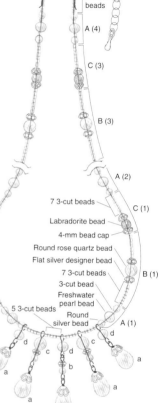

Clasp
Crimp beads
Adjustable chain closure
7 3-cut beads
A (4)
C (3)
B (3)
A (2)
7 3-cut beads
C (1)
Labradorite bead
4-mm bead cap
Round rose quartz bead
Flat silver designer bead
7 3-cut beads
B (1)
3-cut bead
Freshwater pearl bead
5 3-cut beads
Round silver bead
A (1)
d c d c d
a a b a
a a

Supplies (Necklace)

Rose quartz beads
(5 8 x 12-mm teardrop beads, 8 6-mm round beads)

6 5-mm round labradorite beads

11 5-mm round freshwater pearl beads (pink)

Silver beads (19 4-mm round beads, 14 5-mm flat designer beads,
1 5-mm round designer bead)

176 2-mm 3-cut beads (silver: M 181)

Bead caps (12 4-mm, 5 6-mm)

6 2-cm eyepins

2 crimp beads

Spring clasp

Adjustable chain closure

5 20-cm lengths Artistic Wire (silver)

70cm nylon-coated wire

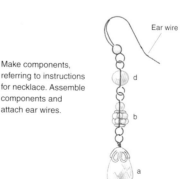

1

Make components and
string on nylon-coated
wire. Add a crimp bead
at each end of necklace.
Attach clasp to one end
and adjustable chain
closure to other.

Components

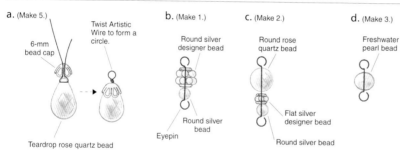

a. (Make 5.)

Twist Artistic
Wire to form a
circle.

6-mm
bead cap

Teardrop rose quartz bead

b. (Make 1.)

Round silver
designer bead

Round silver
bead

Eyepin

c. (Make 2.)

Round rose
quartz bead

Flat silver
designer bead

Round silver bead

d. (Make 3.)

Freshwater
pearl bead

Supplies (Earrings)

2 8 x 12-mm teardrop rose quartz beads

2 5-mm round freshwater pearl beads (pink)

Silver beads (2 4-mm round beads, 2 5-mm round designer beads)

2 6-mm bead caps

4 2-cm eyepins

Ear wires (silver)

2 20-cm lengths Artistic Wire (silver)

Make components,
referring to instructions
for necklace. Assemble
components and
attach ear wires.

Ear wire

d

b

a

PINK AND WHITE NECKLACE & RING

Supplies (Necklace)

Rose quartz beads (64 2-mm round beads, 16 8 x 8.5-mm teardrop beads, 1 11.5 x 16.5-mm teardrop bead)

16 6-mm round coral beads

16 6-mm round freshwater pearl beads (assorted colors)

16 4-mm Swarovski round crystal beads (white alabaster)

1-mm 3-cut beads (128 pink gold: T CRS740), (96 matte pink gold: T CRS551)

2 bead tips
2 crimp beads
3-mm jump ring
Spring clasp
Adjustable chain closure
100cm nylon thread

Supplies (Ring)

2 6-mm round rose quartz beads

2 6-mm round coral beads

4.5-mm round freshwater pearl beads (2 pink, 2 white)

2 4-mm Swarovski round crystal beads (white alabaster)

Round fire-polished beads (21 3-mm beads, 1 4-mm bead) (Capri gold)

54 1-mm 3-cut beads (pink gold: T CRS740)

70cm nylon thread

1
Attach a crimp bead and bead tip to one end of nylon thread, then add beads.

2
Repeat the pattern shown in Step 1, working the two sides in mirror image. Attach a bead tip and a crimp bead. Attach clasp to one end of necklace and adjustable chain closure to other.

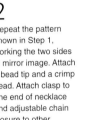

8 x 8.5-mm rose quartz bead

3-cut bead (matte pink gold)

3-cut bead (pink gold)

Bead tip

★

Round Swarovski bead

Coral bead

Round rose quartz bead

Freshwater pearl bead

Crimp bead

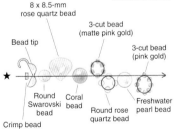

Clasp
Jump ring
Adjustable chain closure

1
2
3
7
8

11.5 x 16.5-mm rose quartz bead

1
Tape nylon thread down to work surface 25cm from one end. String beads, as shown in drawing.

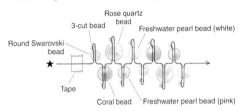

Rose quartz bead

3-cut bead

Freshwater pearl bead (white)

Round Swarovski bead

Tape

Coral bead

Freshwater pearl bead (pink)

2
Remove tape. String and form an intersection in 4-mm fire-polished bead.

4-mm fire-polished bead

3
Make band. Tie threads together and finish off.

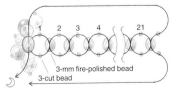

1 2 3 4 21

3-mm fire-polished bead

3-cut bead

Garnet

FLOWER RING & NECKLACE

The lovely flower motif has a calm, relaxing effect due to the deep wine red of the garnet beads used.
Gold beads form the center of the flower. This motif looks beautiful from every angle.

Garnet is the birthstone for January. Its Japanese name means
"pomegranate stone" because of its resemblance to the fruit.
The gemstone is thought to promote vitality, affection and loyalty.

CLOVER WREATH EARRINGS & BRACELET

Four-leaf clovers were the inspiration for this motif.
We fashioned the leaves from very thin leaf-shaped garnet beads, and surrounded them with a wreath-like border.

FLOWER RING & NECKLACE

Supplies (Ring)

8 4 x 6-mm teardrop garnet beads
5-mm round freshwater pearl beads (white)
96 2-mm seed beads (matte gold: M 182)
16 1-mm seed beads (red: M 335)

2 80-cm lengths nylon thread

Supplies (Necklace)

Garnet beads (6 3-mm round beads, 8 4 x 6-mm teardrop beads)
Round freshwater pearl beads (6 3-mm beads, 1 5-mm bead) (white)
44 2-mm seed beads (matte gold: M 182)
322 1-mm seed beads (red: M 335)
320 1-mm 3-cut beads (red: T CRS329)

2 bead tips
2 crimp beads
4-mm jump ring
Spring clasp
Adjustable chain closure
Nylon thread (1 20-cm length, 3 80-cm lengths)

1

Make motif, beginning by stringing beads on center of nylon thread.

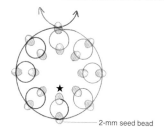

2-mm seed bead

2

Add garnet and 1-mm seed beads. Set one end of thread aside, after working 1 round. With other end, work around perimeter of motif. Tie thread to end previously set aside.

Set this end aside.

Garnet bead
2 1-mm seed beads

3

String freshwater pearl bead on center of a new length of nylon thread. Pass thread through center of motif, then form an intersection in 2-mm seed beads.

Freshwater pearl bead

2-mm seed beads

4

Weave band with same thread. Tie threads together and finish off.

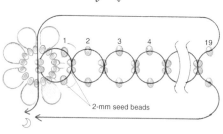

2-mm seed beads

1

Make motif, followings Steps 1-2 of instructions for ring. String a 5-mm freshwater pearl bead on 20-cm length nylon thread and make central section.

5-mm freshwater pearl bead

2 2-mm seed beads

2

Pick up 2 1-mm seed beads on motif with 80cm nylon thread. Add more beads. Tape ends down to work surface. String beads on remaining length of nylon thread. String a crimp bead and bead tip on each end of 2-strand necklace. Attach clasp to one end of necklace and adjustable chain closure to other.

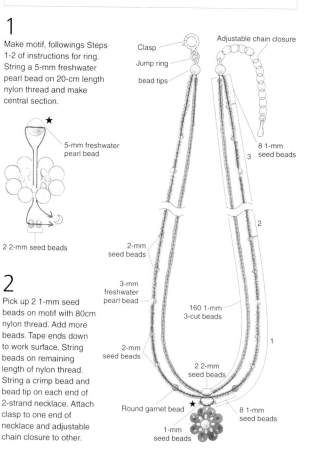

Clasp
Jump ring
bead tips

Adjustable chain closure

8 1-mm seed beads

3

2

2-mm seed beads

3-mm freshwater pearl beads

2-mm seed beads

160 1-mm 3-cut beads

2 2-mm seed beads

1

Round garnet bead

8 1-mm seed beads

1-mm seed beads

10 CLOVER WREATH EARRINGS & BRACELET

Supplies (Earrings)

Garnet beads (4 4-mm round beads, 8 5 x 5-mm teardrop beads)

56 2-mm 3-cut beads (bronze: T CR221)

4 2-cm eyepins

2 4-mm jump rings

Ear wires

2 50-cm lengths nylon thread

Supplies (Bracelet)

Garnet beads (12 4-mm round beads, 12 5 x 5-mm teardrop beads)

84 2-mm 3-cut beads (bronze: T CR221)

12 2-cm eyepins

Jump rings (1 3-mm, 6 4-mm)

Spring clasp

Adjustable chain closure

3 50-cm lengths nylon thread

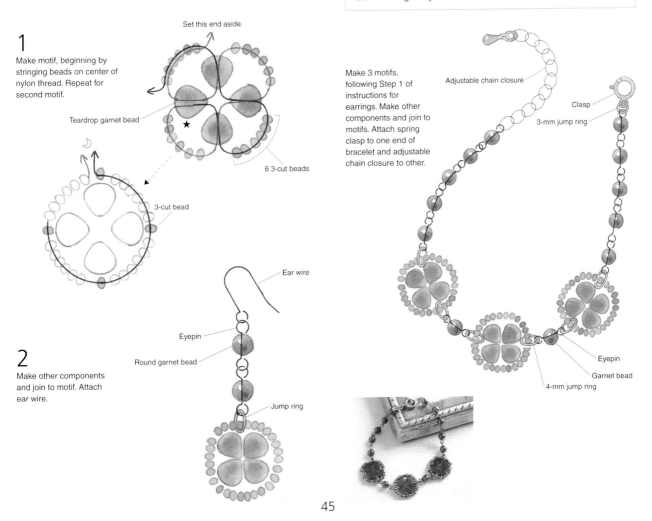

1

Make motif, beginning by stringing beads on center of nylon thread. Repeat for second motif.

Set this end aside.

Teardrop garnet bead

6 3-cut beads

3-cut bead

2

Make other components and join to motif. Attach ear wire.

Ear wire

Eyepin

Round garnet bead

Jump ring

Make 3 motifs, following Step 1 of instructions for earrings. Make other components and join to motifs. Attach spring clasp to one end of bracelet and adjustable chain closure to other.

Adjustable chain closure

Clasp

3-mm jump ring

Eyepin

Garnet bead

4-mm jump ring

45

Freshwater Pearls

PURE NECKLACE & RING

The flower motif made with white teardrop freshwater pearl beads is a symbol of purity and innocence.
The foundation of these delicate pieces is made of 3-cut beads, upon which flower petals are woven.

Pearls, also known as mermaid's tears, are the birthstone for
June. Freshwater pearls are said to enhance feminine charms.
They come in a wide range of colors and shapes.

G R A C E F U L   N E C K L A C E

The small flowers made from rice-shaped freshwater pearl beads add a feminine touch to this piece.
The two-strand necklace adds interest to a simple design.

PURE NECKLACE & RING

Supplies (Necklace)

Freshwater pearl beads (24 3 x 4.5-mm top side-drilled beads (gray), 16 4-mm round beads (white), 7 6-mm round beads (gray), 6 10 x 13-mm teardrop beads (white))

32 3-mm Swarovski bicone crystal beads (crystal)

6 4-mm round fire-polished beads (crystal)

212 2-mm 3-cut beads (white: T CR122)

2 crimp beads

Spring clasp

Adjustable chain closure

Nylon thread (1 20-cm length, 1 100-cm length)

80cm nylon-coated wire

1

Make motif by stringing fire-polished beads on 100cm nylon thread. Form an intersection in first bead strung.

★ Fire-polished bead

2

Add 3-cut beads. When you have strung one round, form an intersection in a 3-cut bead.

13 3-cut beads

3-cut bead

3

Add teardrop freshwater pearl beads onto foundation made in Step 2. Tie threads and finish off.

Teardrop freshwater pearl bead

4

String a freshwater pearl bead on center of 20cm nylon thread to form center of motif. Tie threads.

Round freshwater pearl bead (gray)

5

Thread nylon-coated wire through nylon thread on back of motif, then add beads. Add a crimp bead at each end of necklace. Attach clasp to one end and adjustable chain closure to other.

Patterns

A.

3-cut bead

Bicone bead   Round freshwater pearl bead (white)

B. Top side-drilled freshwater pearl bead

3 3-cut beads

C. Round freshwater pearl bead (gray)

3 3-cut beads

Crimp bead

Clasp   Adjustable chain closure

3 3-cut beads

A

B

A

3

(Enlargement)

Nylon thread

(Back view)

3 3-cut beads

A

B   A   C

1

3

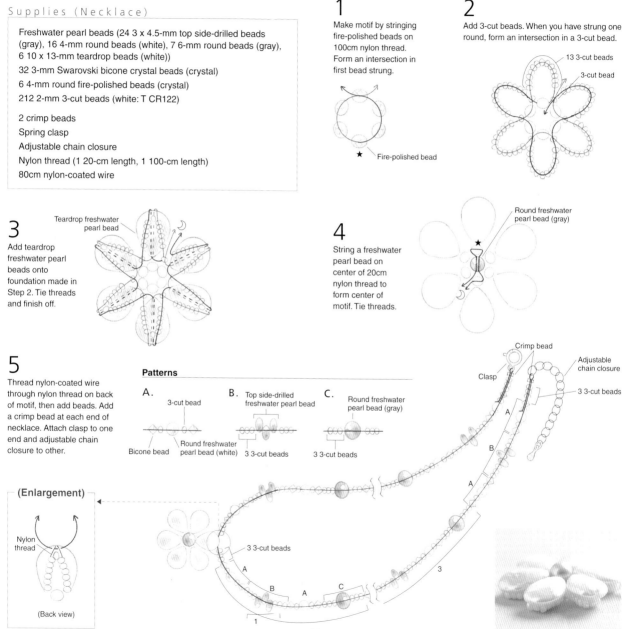

Supplies (Ring)

Freshwater pearl beads (1 4-mm round bead (gray),
4 10 x 13-mm beads (white))

4 3-mm Swarovski bicone crystal beads (crystal)

146 2-mm 3-cut beads (white: T CR122)

2 80-cm lengths nylon thread

1

String bicone
beads on nylon
thread to form
a circle. Add 3-
cut beads.

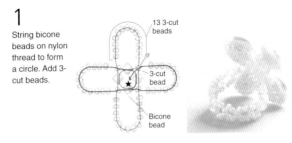

13 3-cut beads

3-cut bead

Bicone bead

2

Add teardrop
freshwater pearl
beads onto
foundation made in
Step 1. Tie threads
and finish off.

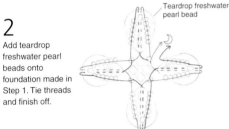

Teardrop freshwater
pearl bead

3

String beads on
center of a new length
of nylon thread. Form
an intersection at back
of motif. Weave band,
tie threads and finish
off.

Round freshwater
pearl bead

2 3-cut beads

3-cut beads

| 1 | 2 | 3 | 4 | 14 | 15 |

GRACEFUL NECKLACE

Supplies

Freshwater pearl beads (7 3.5-mm round beads (pink),
20 6-mm rice beads (assorted colors))

1-mm 3-cut beads (290 matte pink gold: T CRS551,
296 pink gold: T CRS740)

2 bead tips

2 crimp beads

4-mm jump ring

Spring clasp

Adjustable chain closure

Nylon thread (5 30-cm lengths, 2 70-cm lengths)

1

String beads on 30cm
nylon thread to make
motif. You will need 5
motifs in all.

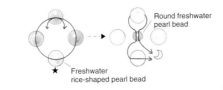

Round freshwater
pearl bead

Freshwater
rice-shaped pearl bead

2

Make necklace,
using 70cm nylon
thread. Add a crimp
bead and bead tip at
each end of
necklace. Attach
clasp to one end and
adjustable chain
closure to other.

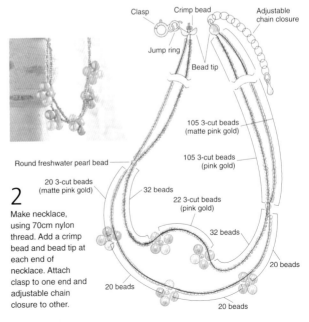

Clasp

Crimp bead

Adjustable
chain closure

Jump ring

Bead tip

105 3-cut beads
(matte pink gold)

105 3-cut beads
(pink gold)

Round freshwater pearl bead

20 3-cut beads
(matte pink gold)

32 beads

22 3-cut beads
(pink gold)

32 beads

20 beads

20 beads

20 beads

Carnelian

NATURAL NECKLACE

We were delighted to find flower-shaped carnelian beads, and combined three of them to make the motif.
For the necklace, we chose a simple design that requires only stringing chip carnelian beads on wire. This gemstone lends itself well to simple designs.

Napoleon I was apparently very fond of an octagonal carnelian seal.
Carnelian is believed to have the power to motivate, to make dreams come
true and to give us courage. Wearing carnelian is said to ensure victory.

B L O O M I N G   N E C K L A C E   &   B R O O C H

Since there is so much variation among carnelians, no piece of jewelry made with carnelian beads can ever be monochrome.
Enjoy the way the color changes when they reflect light.

NATURAL NECKLACE

Supplies

Carnelian beads
(3 3-mm round beads, 18 4-mm chip beads, 3 15-mm flower beads)
36 4-mm chip citrine beads
10 4-mm chip smoky quartz beads
8 6-mm round red aventurine beads
36 3-mm round fire-polished beads (smoke topaz)
127 2-mm seed beads (brown: M301)

2 crimp beads
Spring clasp
Adjustable chain closure
60cm nylon thread
70cm nylon-coated wire

1

Make motif, stringing seed beads and carnelian flower beads on nylon thread.

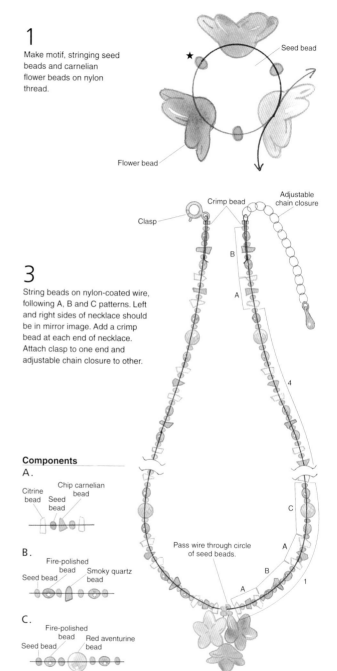

Seed bead

Flower bead

2

Add seed beads and round carnelian beads. Add seed beads on perimeter, then tie threads and finish off.

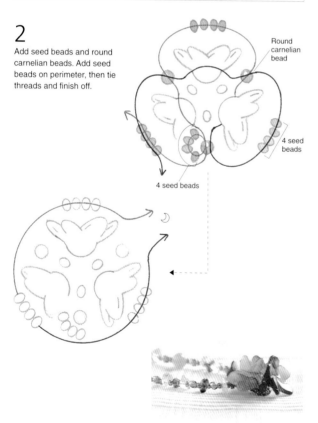

Round carnelian bead

4 seed beads

4 seed beads

3

String beads on nylon-coated wire, following A, B and C patterns. Left and right sides of necklace should be in mirror image. Add a crimp bead at each end of necklace. Attach clasp to one end and adjustable chain closure to other.

Clasp

Crimp bead

Adjustable chain closure

B

A

4

Pass wire through circle of seed beads.

C

A

B

A

1

Components

A.

Citrine bead
Seed bead
Chip carnelian bead

B.

Seed bead
Fire-polished bead
Smoky quartz bead

C.

Seed bead
Fire-polished bead
Red aventurine bead

52

BLOOMING NECKLACE & BROOCH

Petal-shaped carnelian beads
(6 11 x 15-mm beads, 6 13 x 17-mm beads)

Botswana agate button beads
(8 5 x 8-mm beads, 4 6 x 10-mm beads)

6-mm round freshwater pearl bead (beige)

36 2-mm 3-cut beads (orange: M1277)

12 2-cm eyepins

4 3-mm jump rings

14 2.5-cm lengths designer chain

Perforated finding (15mm diameter)

Spring clasp

Adjustable chain closure

2 60-cm lengths nylon thread

1

Make motif, beginning by stringing beads on center of nylon thread. Close circle. Pass thread through 3-cut beads. Tie threads and finish off.

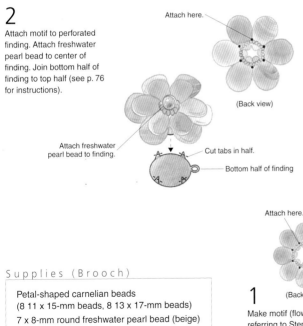

13 x 17-mm carnelian bead

11 x 15-mm carnelian bead

4 3-cut beads

2 3-cut beads

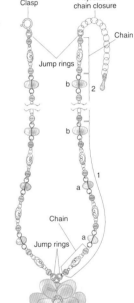

Clasp

Adjustable chain closure

Chain

Jump rings

b

2

b

1

Chain

a

a

Jump rings

2

Attach motif to perforated finding. Attach freshwater pearl bead to center of finding. Join bottom half of finding to top half (see p. 76 for instructions).

Attach here.

Attach freshwater pearl bead to finding.

(Back view)

Cut tabs in half.

Bottom half of finding

3

Join components and designer chain to make necklace. Attach clasp to one end and adjustable chain closure to other with jump rings.

Components

a. (Make 8.)

Eyepin

5 x 8-mm Botswana agate bead

b. (Make 4.)

6 x 10-mm Botswana agate bead

Petal-shaped carnelian beads
(8 11 x 15-mm beads, 8 13 x 17-mm beads)

7 x 8-mm round freshwater pearl bead (beige)

90 2-mm 3-cut beads (orange: M1277)

Perforated brooch back (20mm diameter)

2 80-cm lengths nylon thread

Attach here.

(Back view)

1

Make motif (flower with 8 petals), referring to Step 1 of instructions for necklace. Attach to perforated brooch back (see Step 2 of instructions for necklace).

2

Pass thread through to front of brooch back. String 42 3-cut beads on thread. Wind thread around base of motif. Secure motif to brooch back.

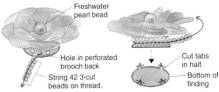

Freshwater pearl bead

Hole in perforated brooch back

String 42 3-cut beads on thread.

Cut tabs in half.

Bottom of finding

Turquoise

FRINGED SILVER NECKLACE & CROSS NECKLACE

Silver and turquoise have always gone well together, but the combination tends to get lumped into the ethnic category.
We gave it a fresh look with fringe and a cross design.

Turquoise is the birthstone for December. The name means "Turkish stone" (turquoise reached Europe from Egypt via Turkey). Legend has it that turquoise keeps travelers safe and strengthens friendships.

D O M E   N E C K L A C E   &   R I N G

We arranged turquoise button beads and fire-polished beads into a dome, and placed a larger turquoise bead in the center. We chose a simple, classic two-strand design for the necklace.

FRINGED SILVER NECKLACE & CROSS NECKLACE

Supplies (Fringed Necklace)

3 8-mm round turquoise beads
3 4.5 x 8-mm button mother-of-pearl beads
3 7.5 x 12-mm teardrop smoky quartz beads
60 2-mm seed beads (silver: M181)
6 3-mm seed beads (silver: M 181)

3 2-cm eyepins
Jump rings (3 3-mm, 8 4-mm)
2 side-clamp bead tips
53cm 1.5-mm (diameter) ball chain
Spring clasp
Adjustable chain closure
3 20-cm lengths Artistic Wire
3 60-cm lengths nylon thread

Supplies (Cross Necklace)

Turquoise beads (20 3.5 x 6-mm lozenge beads,
10 3.5 x 8-mm oval beads, 4 8-mm round beads)
8 8 x 10-mm oval carnelian beads
16 4-mm round fire-polished beads (jet AB)
80 2-mm seed beads (silver (M181))
3-mm seed beads (4 blue: T82), (28 silver: M181)

54 2-cm eyepins
2 4-mm jump rings
Spring clasp
Adjustable chain closure
Nylon thread (1 30-cm length, 4 60-cm lengths)

1

String beads on nylon thread to make motif.

Turquoise bead

2-mm seed bead ★

2

String 3-mm seed beads to form opposite ends of motif. Tie threads and finish off. Make 3 of these motifs.

3-mm seed bead

8 2-mm seed beads

3

Attach a jump ring to each end of motif. Make other components, using Artistic Wire, and join to motifs. To make necklace, pass ball chain through jump rings and add a bead tip to each end (see p. 77 for instructions). Attach clasp to one end and adjustable chain closure to other with jump rings.

4-mm jump rings

Clasp

Bead tips

Adjustable chain closure

Chain

3-mm jump ring

4-mm jump rings

Leave a 1-cm space here.

Motif

Mother-of-pearl bead

Eyepin

Smoky quartz bead

Twist wire.

1

Make 4 motifs, referring to Steps 1-2 of instructions for fringed necklace. Join motifs with 30cm nylon thread.

3-mm seed bead (blue)

2

Make Components a and b, using eyepins. Join components, referring to drawings, to make necklace. Attach clasp to one end and adjustable chain closure to other with jump rings.

Components

a.

Lozenge turquoise bead

Button turquoise bead

3-mm seed bead (silver)

Eyepin

(Make 10.)

b.

Fire-polished bead

Carnelian bead

(Make 8.)

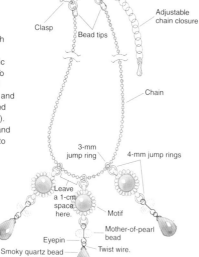

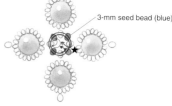

Adjustable chain closure

Clasp

Jump rings

a (5)

a (2)

b (1)

Jump ring

a (1)

DOME NECKLACE & RING

Supplies (Necklace)

Turquoise beads (10 1.5 x 4-mm button beads,
4 5-mm round beads, 1 9-mm round bead)
14 3 x 5-mm button fire-polished beads (green turquoise)
Swarovski bicone crystal beads
(4 green ultramarine, 6 light Colorado topaz)
2-mm seed beads (20 brown: M311), (240 green: H935)
40 2-mm 3-cut beads (gold: T CR712)
294 1-mm 3-cut beads (green: T CRS180)

2 crimp beads
4-mm jump ring
Spring clasp
Adjustable chain closure
80cm nylon thread
2 60-cm lengths nylon-coated wire

Supplies (Ring)

Turquoise beads (10 1.5 x 4-mm button beads, 1 9-mm round bead)
10 3 x 5-mm button fire-polished beads (green turquoise)
13 3-mm round fire-polished beads (bronze)
2-mm seed beads (20 brown: M311), (68 green: H935)
20 2-mm 3-cut beads (gold: T CR712)

Nylon thread (1 60-cm length, 1 80-cm length)

Make motif, following directions in Steps
1-3 of instructions for necklace. Weave
band, using 60cm nylon thread and
picking up beads from motif. Tie threads
and finish off.

1

Make motif, beginning by stringing
beads on center of nylon thread.
Close circle.

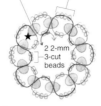

Fire-polished bead
4 2-mm seed beads (green)
2 2-mm 3-cut beads

2

String turquoise beads and 2-mm
seed beads, picking up 2-mm 3-cut
beads as you go along.

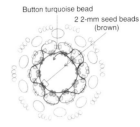

Button turquoise bead
2 2-mm seed beads (brown)

3

Add 9-mm turquoise bead at
center of motif. Run thread back
through beads on perimeter. Tie
threads and finish off.

9-mm turquoise bead

4

Attach jump ring to 2-mm seed
beads on outer edge of motif.
String beads on nylon-coated wire.
Left and right sides should be in
mirror image. Add a crimp bead at
each end of necklace. Attach clasp
to one end and adjustable chain
closure to other.

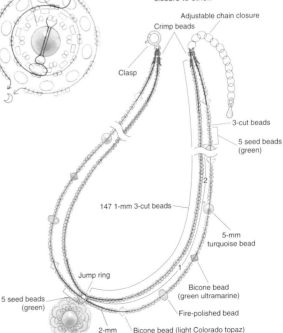

Adjustable chain closure
Crimp beads
Clasp
3-cut beads
5 seed beads (green)
147 1-mm 3-cut beads
5-mm turquoise bead
Jump ring
Bicone bead (green ultramarine)
Fire-polished bead
5 seed beads (green)
2-mm 3-cut bead
Bicone bead (light Colorado topaz)

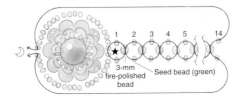

1 2 3 4 5 14
3-mm fire-polished bead
Seed bead (green)

Labradorite

LAVENDER NECKLACE

When light shines through the motif, which combines labradorite with amethyst beads,
the effect is almost unearthly.

Labradorite

This gemstone does not come in gaudy colors, but when it reflects light, a magical rainbow effect results. Labradorite is said to protect the person who owns it, and to temper harmful emotions like anger and jealousy.

DOME NECKLACE & RING

We arranged turquoise button beads and fire-polished beads into a dome, and placed a larger turquoise bead in the center.
We chose a simple, classic two-strand design for the necklace.

LAVENDER NECKLACE

Supplies

Round labradorite beads (16 3-mm beads, 29 5-mm beads)

7 4 x 7-mm button amethyst beads

19 3-mm button freshwater pearl beads (blue-gray)

12 3-mm Swarovski round crystal beads (crystal VM)

2-mm 3-cut beads (12 gold: T CR712), (188 green: T CR539)

2 crimp beads

Spring clasp

Adjustable chain closure

80cm nylon thread

70cm nylon-coated wire

1

Make motif, beginning by stringing beads on center of nylon thread.

★

5-mm labradorite bead

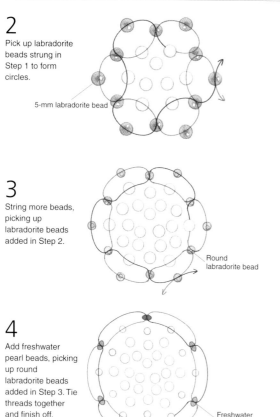

2

Pick up labradorite beads strung in Step 1 to form circles.

5-mm labradorite bead

3

String more beads, picking up labradorite beads added in Step 2.

Round labradorite bead

4

Add freshwater pearl beads, picking up round labradorite beads added in Step 3. Tie threads together and finish off.

Freshwater pearl bead

5

Thread nylon-coated wire under a working thread at back of motif. Make necklace. Add a crimp bead at each end of necklace. Attach clasp to one end and adjustable chain closure to other.

Patterns

A.

3-mm labradorite bead

3-cut beads (green)

10 3-cut beads (green)

5-mm labradorite bead

B.

10 3-cut beads (green)

3-cut bead (gold)

Amethyst bead

Freshwater pearl bead

3-cut bead (green)

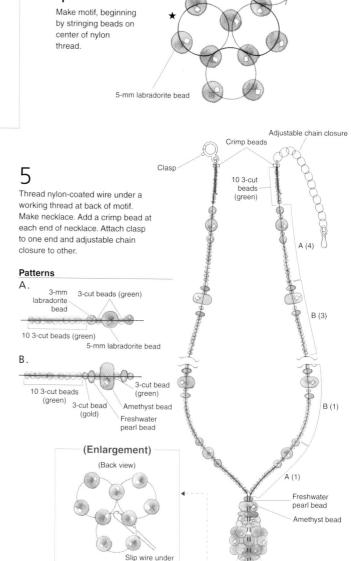

Clasp

Crimp beads

Adjustable chain closure

10 3-cut beads (green)

A (4)

B (3)

B (1)

A (1)

Freshwater pearl bead

Amethyst bead

(Enlargement)

(Back view)

Slip wire under working thread.

60

PAIRED RINGS

Supplies

2 8 x 10-mm oval labradorite beads

166 2-mm seed beads (silver: M181)

4 60-cm lengths nylon thread

1

Make motif, beginning by stringing beads on center of nylon thread. Form an intersection in a seed bead.

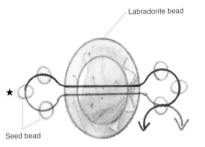

Labradorite bead

★

Seed bead

2

Add more seed beads, working around perimeter of motif.

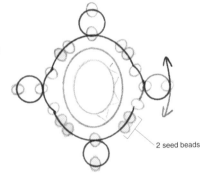

2 seed beads

3

String more seed beads. Tie threads together and finish off.

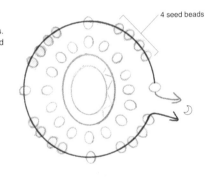

4 seed beads

4

With a new length of nylon thread, pick up seed beads in motif and weave band. Tie threads together and finish off. Repeat these steps for second ring.

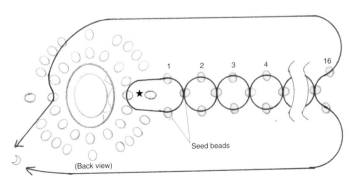

★

1 2 3 4   16

Seed beads

(Back view)

61

Gemstones

The subtle differences in color, brilliance and transparency among the many types of gemstones are what makes them so seductive. Here we introduce some of the gemstones used for the jewelry in this book, as well as the powers attributed to them.

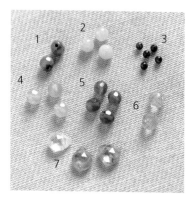

1. **Malachite:** Color of peacock feathers; symbol of long life and prosperity
2. **Chrysoprase:** Translucent green quartz: said to build confidence
3. **Green sandstone:** Deep green stone with gold streaks
4. **Green aventurine:** Brings good luck to gamblers
5. **Green agate:** Helps build good relationships; enhances creative and analytical powers
6. **Peridot:** Known as the gem of the sun: wards off evil spirits
7. **Grossular garnet:** Pale green, pale yellow or white gemstone

1. **Coral:** Known as the "elixir of life" in Japan
2. **Red agate:** Brings its wearer victory; promotes good relationships
3. **Opal:** Called "Cupid's stone;" gives hope

1. **Aquamarine:** A type of emerald referred to as the "sea nymph"
2. **Blue quartz:** Enhances intuitive capabilities and dispels gloom
3. **Blue sandstone:** Dark blue stone with gold streaks; promotes friendships
4. **Lavender amethyst:** Has a calming, harmonious effect
5. **Amethyst:** Enhances attractiveness; prevents excessive eating and drinking
6. **Amazonite:** Type of moonstone; called the "stone of hope"

1. **Fire opal:** Referred to as the "rainbow stone;" nurtures love
2. **Cubic zirconia:** Synthetic stone with the brilliance of diamonds
3. **Amber:** Has magical powers of attraction; improves sociability
4. **Citrine:** November birthstone; improves financial fortunes and friendships
5. **Gold sandstone:** Brown gemstone with gold streaks; heightens confidence
6. **Sapphire:** This "royal gem" provides wisdom and creativity
7. **Red aventurine:** Variety of quartz that calms the nerves
8. **Botswana agate:** Revered in Botswana for its protective powers; has relaxing effect

1. **Mother of pearl:** Interior shell of an oyster; promotes happy marriages and rewards diligence
2. **Onyx:** Often used for rosary beads; protects wearers and brings them good luck
3. **Rainbow moonstone:** Type of feldspar that glows like the moon; protects travelers, cleanses mind and body, and alleviates sadness
4. **Howlite:** Purifies mind and body; has a cheering effect
5. **Smoky quartz:** Cures fatigue and stabilizes moods

COMBINATION PATTERNS

It's possible to completely transform a motif, by changing the colors of the beads, or color placement, or by varying the design of the necklace attached to it. Here we introduce three patterns. We hope they, along with some advice we offer, will inspire you to create original jewelry.

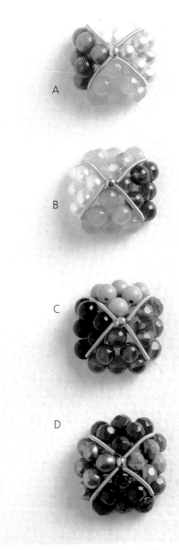

A

B

C

D

Pattern 1
Four-Color Combination

Some four-color combinations look gaudy or even random, two eventualities we usually want to avoid. The best way to arrive at a good color combination is to decide on the first color you wish to use. Then choose the color you wish to place next to it, and so on.

Take Pattern B, for instance. To create it, we placed yellow beads next to purple beads (yellow is the complementary color of purple). Next we chose lavender and white, since they go nicely with both yellow and purple. Complementary colors and colors of the same family go together well, as do achromatic black and white.

Gold coil (or French wire) is instrumental in making these four-color combinations work, since gold harmonizes with every other color.

By placing the coil between sections of the motif, you unify it.

A. Orange and green, reflected in two shades of white
B. Purple and yellow (a combination commonly used in traditional Japanese arts and crafts)
C. Color arrangement designed to showcase the turquoise beads
D. Gold and dark red add a note of sophistication to the two types of blue beads

Variations: Ring & Necklace   p.65

Matching pieces are a wonderful idea for this simple design. For the ring, we made very minor changes to the color arrangement.

Color Variations

Supplies (Motif B)

6 4-mm round red aventurine beads

6 4-mm round amethyst beads

6 4-mm round lavender amethyst beads

6 4-mm round freshwater pearl beads (white)

2-mm metal bead (gold)

4 1-cm lengths 0.6mm (inner diameter) coil or French wire

60cm nylon thread

Supplies (Motif C)

6 4-mm round green agate beads

6 4-mm round turquoise beads

6 4-mm round onyx beads

6 4-mm round amber beads

2-mm metal bead (gold)

4 1-cm lengths 0.6mm (inner diameter) coil or French wire

60cm nylon thread

Supplies (Motif D)

6 4-mm round freshwater pearl beads (gold)

6 4-mm round blue sandstone beads

6 4-mm round malachite beads

6 4-mm round red agate beads

2-mm metal bead (gold)

4 1-cm lengths 0.6mm (inner diameter) coil or French wire

60cm nylon thread

MAKING THE MOTIF

Supplies (Motif A)

6 4-mm round coral beads

6 4-mm round green aventurine beads

6 4-mm round freshwater pearl beads (pink)

6 4-mm round cat's-eye beads (white)

2-mm metal bead (gold)

4 1-cm lengths 0.6mm (inner diameter) coil or French wire

60cm nylon thread

1

Begin stringing beads on center of nylon thread, working in mirror image.

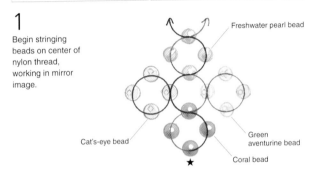

Freshwater pearl bead

Cat's-eye bead

Green aventurine bead

Coral bead

★

2

Work around perimeter of motif, as shown in drawing. Pull threads to form

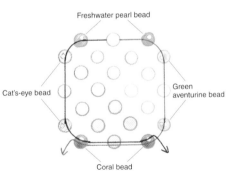

Freshwater pearl bead

Cat's-eye bead

Green aventurine bead

Coral bead

3

Add coil and metal bead. Tie threads together and finish off.

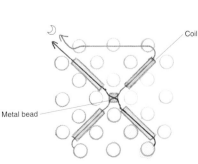

Coil

Metal bead

VARIATION:
RING

Supplies (in addition to beads for motif)

41 2-mm metal beads (gold)

60cm nylon thread

Make motif, switching positions of cat's-eye and green aventurine beads. Weave band. Tie threads together and finish off.

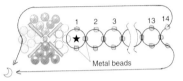

Metal beads

VARIATION:
NECKLACE

Supplies (in addition to beads for motif)

4 4-mm round coral beads

4 4-mm round green aventurine beads

4 4-mm round freshwater pearl beads (pink)

4 4-mm round cat's-eye beads (white)

162 2-mm metal beads (gold)

2 crimp beads

3-mm jump ring

Spring clasp

Adjustable chain closure

60cm nylon-coated wire

Make motif. Attach a jump ring to motif. String beads on nylon-coated wire. Add a crimp bead at each end of necklace. Attach clasp to one end and adjustable chain closure to other.

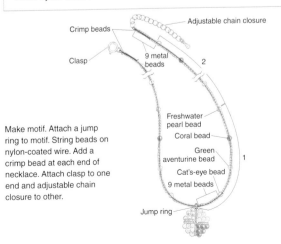

Adjustable chain closure

Crimp beads

Clasp

9 metal beads

Freshwater pearl bead

Coral bead

Green aventurine bead

Cat's-eye bead

9 metal beads

Jump ring

Pattern 2
Layered Colors

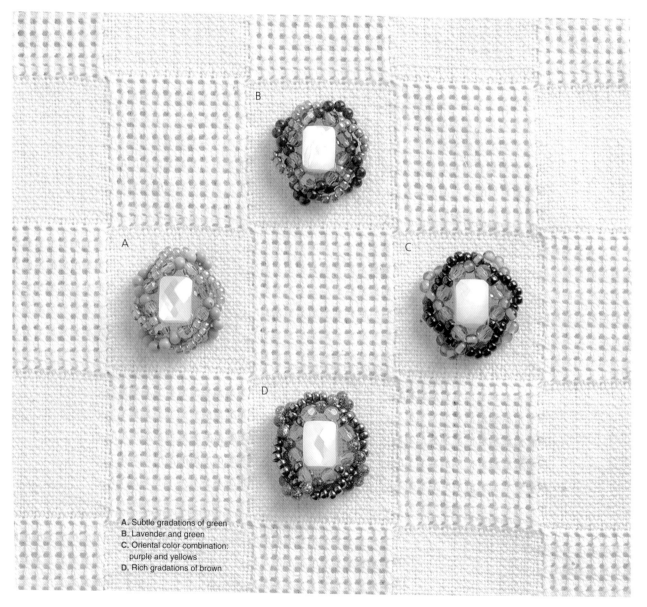

A. Subtle gradations of green
B. Lavender and green
C. Oriental color combination:
   purple and yellows
D. Rich gradations of brown

Variation: Necklace   p.68

The turquoise beads in the
necklace and motif unite
the entire piece.

This motif features a square mother-of-pearl bead surrounded by intertwined ropes of beads in two colors. When your motif has a complex design, it's best to choose colors that are in the same family (as in Motifs A and D), so that the piece doesn't look too busy. For Motif A, I opted for a soft effect, surrounding the central mother-of pearl bead with pale green round beads, and selecting green seed beads and round turquoise beads for the twisted ropes. Using complementary colors for the twisted ropes (like the green in B and the yellow in C), emphasizes the design. Another possibility is replacing the mother-of-pearl bead with a bead of a different color or shape. In that case, it's a good idea to avoid using beads in the same color family as the central bead for the twisted ropes, since doing so would lessen the effect of the twisted rope design.

When you make a motif with several layers, try arranging beads in a tray or other work surface to see how they look from a distance before you actually string them. If you like the way they look then, chances are good that you'll still like them later on.

Variation: Ring   p.68

We used the same
soft greens and blues
for the band.

MAKING THE MOTIF

Supplies (A)

6 x 8-mm cube mother-of pearl bead with 2 holes (white)
28 2-mm round turquoise beads
8 3-mm Swarovski round crystal beads (peridot satin)
40 2-mm seed beads (white: H935)

80cm nylon thread

1

Weave figure eights, beginning at center of nylon thread.

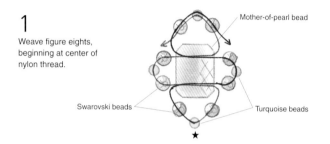

Mother-of-pearl bead

Swarovski beads

Turquoise beads

★

2

Add seed beads. Set one end of thread aside.

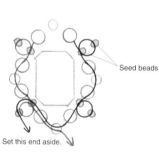

Seed beads

Set this end aside.

3

String turquoise beads on other end of thread to make perimeter of motif. String seed beads on thread end set aside previously to make remainder of perimeter. Tie threads together and finish off.

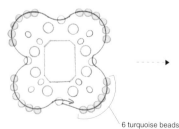

6 turquoise beads

8 seed beads

VARIATION:

RING

Supplies (in addition to beads for motif)

11 2-mm round turquoise beads
48 2-mm seed beads (green: H935)

80cm nylon thread

Make band with new length of nylon thread. Tie threads together and finish off.

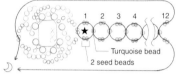

1 2 3 4   12

Turquoise bead

2 seed beads

VARIATION:

NECKLACE

Supplies (in addition to beads for motif)

204 2-mm round turquoise beads

2 crimp beads
6-mm jump ring
Spring clasp
Adjustable chain closure
80cm nylon-coated wire

Attach a jump ring to a seed bead in motif. String beads on nylon-coated wire. Add a crimp bead at each end of necklace. Attach clasp to one end and adjustable chain closure to other.

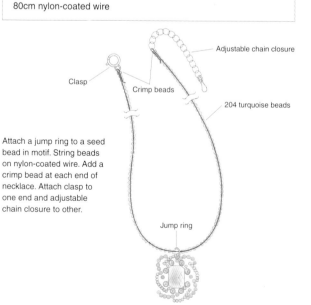

Adjustable chain closure

Clasp

Crimp beads

204 turquoise beads

Jump ring

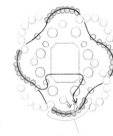

Color Variations

Supplies (Motif B)

6 x 8-mm cube mother-of pearl bead with 2 holes (white)

28 2-mm round green sandstone beads

8 3-mm Swarovski round crystal beads (rose satin)

40 2-mm seed beads (purple: T960)

80cm nylon thread

Supplies (Motif C)

6 x 8-mm cube mother-of pearl bead with 2 holes (white)

28 2-mm round amber beads

8 3-mm Swarovski round crystal beads (tanzanite)

40 2-mm seed beads (iris purple: M454)

80cm nylon thread

Supplies (Motif D)

6 x 8-mm cube mother-of pearl bead with 2 holes (white)

28 2-mm round gold sandstone beads

8 3-mm Swarovski round crystal beads (light Colorado topaz)

40 2-mm seed beads (bronze: M457)

80cm nylon thread

Color Advice

1 Choose your favorite color for the main color

You'll enjoy making jewelry more if you choose colors you like. And you're bound to like a piece that combines different shades of your favorite color.

2 Study the colors of flowers and plants

Books about antiques, plants and flowers are wonderful references for color combinations. Study the gradations of color in petals and the composition of flower paintings. Jewelry inspired by color combinations found in Nature is bound to be beautiful.

3 Don't be afraid of random arrangements

When I'm searching for a new color combination, I often find myself making random arrangements of beads and then studying them. More often than not, I'll hit upon a combination that seems just right. Then I determine the basic color pattern by adding other shades of the same color, or complementary colors.

COMBINING COMPONENTS

Silk thread

Chain

Nylon-coated wire
(double strand)

Pin

Leather cord

Nylon-coated wire
(single strand)

Once you've made a motif you like, you'll want to give just as much thought to the necklace (or bracelet band) to which it will be attached. Just rely on your imagination, and you're sure to come up with several possibilities. You may be planning to wear the jewelry you make with a particular style of fashion. In that case, your decisions will be influenced by that style.

I designed six necklaces to go with this motif. The simple, traditional necklace made by stringing beads on nylon-coated wire creates a serene, muted impression. Necklaces fashioned from linked headpins or eyepins and beads are reminiscent of antiques. Necklaces strung on silk thread are suggestive of the Orient.

Color arrangements are just as important as the materials you select. If you use the same color beads in the necklace as in the motif, you have overall harmony. For an elegant look, make a thin necklace (even one with two strands) to go with a large motif.

Garnet pairs beautifully with gold or bronze.
The motif comes to life when framed in bugle beads.
(My necklace designs begin on p. 72.)

MAKING THE MOTIF

Supplies

10 4-mm round garnet beads
10 2-mm round gold sandstone beads
8-mm round mother-of-pearl bead
10 4-mm round glass beads (beige)
40 1-mm seed beads (bronze: T221)
10 6-mm bugle beads (reddish brown: T222)
100cm nylon thread

1

String beads on center of nylon thread to form a circle. Close circle.

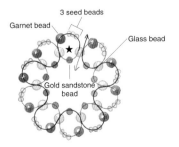

3 seed beads
Garnet bead
Glass bead
Gold sandstone bead

2

Add bugle beads, picking up beads strung in Step 1 as you go along. Add mother-of-pearl bead at center of motif. Tie threads together and finish off.

Bugle bead

Mother-of-pearl bead

SIX VARIATIONS

C. Necklace strung on two strands
The pairs of beads (garnet and glass beads) extending from the necklace serve as accents. The beads for the necklace are strung on two strands of nylon-coated wire.

B. Eyepin necklace
The necklace will look better if the circles formed with pliers at the ends of eyepins are all the same size. Mother-of-pearl beads make opulent accents.

A. Chain necklace
A necklace consisting only of chain wouldn't be an interesting pairing for this motif. For this version, we made short strands of fringe with bugle beads and attached them to the chain.

A. CHAIN NECKLACE

Supplies (in addition to beads for motif)

6 4-mm round garnet beads
18 2-mm round golden sandstone beads
18 1-mm seed beads (bronze: T221)
18 6-mm bugle beads (reddish brown: T222)

24 2-cm headpins
Jump rings (9 4-mm, 1 6-mm)
Chain (6 2.5-cm lengths, 2 16.5-cm lengths)
Spring clasp
Adjustable chain closure

Attach a jump ring to motif. Join components so that left and right sides are in mirror image. Attach clasp to one end of necklace and adjustable chain closure to other with jump rings.

Components

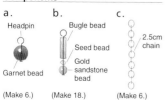

a.
Headpin

Garnet bead

(Make 6.)

b.
Bugle bead

Seed bead

Gold sandstone bead

(Make 18.)

c.
2.5cm chain

(Make 6.)

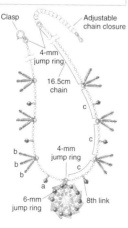

Clasp
Adjustable chain closure
4-mm jump ring
16.5cm chain
c
c
b
b
b
a
4-mm jump ring
c
6-mm jump ring
8th link

B. EYEPIN NECKLACE

Supplies (in addition to beads for motif)

32 4-mm round garnet beads
6 8-mm round mother-of-pearl beads (beige)
8 4-mm round glass beads (beige)
80 1-mm seed beads (bronze: T221)

46 2-cm eyepins
Jump rings (3 4-mm, 1 6-mm)
Spring clasp
Adjustable chain closure

Make components and join, as shown in drawings. Attach clasp to one end of necklace and adjustable chain closure to other with jump rings.

Components

a.
Eyepin

Seed bead

Garnet bead

(Make 32.)

b.
Seed bead

Glass bead

(Make 8.)

c.
Mother-of-pearl bead

(Make 6.)

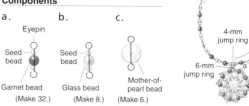

Clasp
Adjustable chain closure
4
4-mm jump ring
2
c
a
a
4-mm jump ring
1
a
b
a
6-mm jump ring

F. Leather cord necklace
Leather cord alone creates a rather rigid impression, so we softened the look by adding small bead clusters.

E. Silk thread necklace
This is a simple design: you just tie garnet beads onto silk thread. The silk thread creates an opulent Oriental atmosphere.

D. Necklace strung on one strand of wire
This is probably the most commonly used technique: stringing beads on one strand of nylon-coated wire. But we added interest by alternating large and small beads.

C. NECKLACE STRUNG ON TWO STRANDS OF WIRE

Supplies (in addition to beads for motif)

16 4-mm round garnet beads
28 2-mm round golden sandstone beads
14 4-mm round glass beads (beige)
324 1-mm seed beads (bronze: T221)

2 crimp beads
6-mm jump ring
Spring clasp
Adjustable chain closure
2 70-cm strands nylon-coated wire

Attach a jump ring to motif and pass both strands nylon-coated wire through jump ring. String beads, following directions in drawings. Add a crimp bead at each end of necklace. Attach clasp to one end and adjustable chain

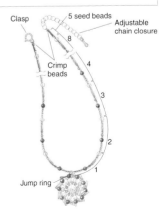

Clasp
7
Adjustable chain closure
3
Crimp beads
2
1
Garnet beads
Jump ring
15 seed beads

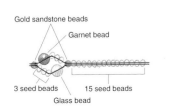

Gold sandstone beads
Garnet bead
3 seed beads
15 seed beads
Glass bead

D. NECKLACE STRUNG ON SINGLE STRAND OF WIRE

Supplies (in addition to beads for motif)

16 4-mm round garnet beads
16 2-mm round gold sandstone beads
16 4-mm glass beads (beige)
138 1-mm seed beads (bronze: T221)
16 6-mm bugle beads (reddish brown: T222)

2 crimp beads
6-mm jump ring
Spring clasp
Adjustable chain closure
70cm nylon-coated wire

Attach a jump ring to motif, and pass nylon-coated wire through jump ring. String beads, following directions in drawings. Add a crimp bead at each end of necklace. Attach clasp to one end and adjustable chain closure to other.

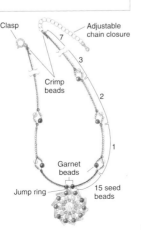

Clasp
5 seed beads
Adjustable chain closure
8
Crimp beads
4
3
2
1
Jump ring

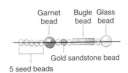

Garnet bead
Bugle bead
Glass bead
Gold sandstone bead
5 seed beads

E. NECKLACE STRUNG ON SILK THREAD

Supplies (in addition to beads for motif)

20 4-mm round garnet beads

2 bead tips

2 crimp beads

Jump rings (2 4-mm, 1 6-mm)

Spring clasp

Adjustable chain closure

100cm silk thread (purple)

Quick-drying glue

1

Apply glue to ends of silk thread. When glue is partially set, quickly twist ends of thread between your fingers to narrow them. String a garnet bead on thread and tie thread tightly, referring to drawings.

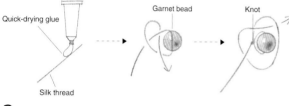

Quick-drying glue

Garnet bead

Knot

Silk thread

2

String garnet beads every 2.5cm, tying each one as in Step 1. Attach a jump ring to motif, and pass thread through jump ring. String a crimp bead and bead tip on each end of necklace. Attach clasp to one end and adjustable chain closure to other.

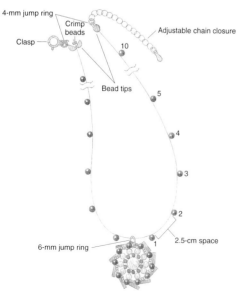

4-mm jump ring

Crimp beads

Clasp

Adjustable chain closure

10

Bead tips

5

4

3

2

6-mm jump ring

2.5-cm space

F. LEATHER CORD NECKLACE

Supplies (in addition to beads for motif)

8 4-mm round garnet beads

4 4-mm round glass beads

12 2-cm headpins

8 crimp beads

Jump rings (2 4-mm, 1 6-mm)

2 cord tips

Spring clasp

Adjustable chain closure

40cm leather cord

Attach a jump ring to motif, and pass leather cord through jump ring. Make components and attach to leather cord, spacing them as shown in drawings. Insert ends of leather cord into cord tips. Attach clasp to one end of necklace and adjustable chain closure to other with jump rings.

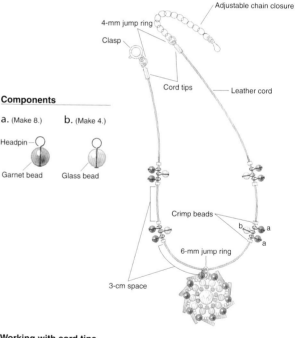

Adjustable chain closure

4-mm jump ring

Clasp

Cord tips

Leather cord

Crimp beads

b

a

a

6-mm jump ring

3-cm space

Components

a. (Make 8.)

Headpin

Garnet bead

b. (Make 4.)

Glass bead

Working with cord tips

1. Insert end of leather cord into cord tip.

2. Crimp cord tip with flat-nose pliers.

3. Closed cord tip

BASIC TECHNIQUES

The first and last steps are crucial to the jewelry-making process. The more skillful you become at these basic techniques, the more beautiful your finished product will be.

WEAVING WITH NYLON THREAD

The figure eight is one of the most common weaving patterns. Keep the thread taut, and be sure to hide all thread ends.

Figure eights

1. String 3 beads on center of thread.

2. Add another bead. Form an intersection in that bead (pass right-hand end of thread through to left, and left-hand end of thread through to right).

3. Add a bead to each end of thread, next to blue bead.

4. Add another bead and form an intersection in it.

5. Pull both threads. Repeat these 5 steps.

CRIMP BEADS

These are attached to the ends of nylon thread or nylon-coated wire to accommodate spring clasps, adjustable chain closures and other findings.

Tying and finishing off threads

1. Tie two ends of thread together.

2. Tie ends 1-2 more times for a secure knot.

3. Hide one end in adjacent beads.

4. Pull thread end so that knot slips inside adjacent bead.

5. Cut excess thread at the edge of a bead.

WORKING WITH FINDINGS

Findings are used when you're finishing off nylon thread or nylon-coated wire, or when you're joining components of a piece of jewelry. Here we demonstrate how some of the most common findings are used.

CRIMP BEADS

These are attached to the ends of nylon thread or nylon-coated wire to accommodate spring clasps, adjustable chain closures and other findings.

PERFORATED FINDINGS

These convenient items are designed for brooches, earrings and necklaces. They have two parts: a top half with holes for attaching beads, and a bottom half with tabs that fit into slots in the top half.

Attaching a spring clasp

1. String a crimp bead, then a spring clasp on end of nylon-coated wire.

2. Pass end of wire back through crimp bead and 2 additional beads, forming a circle.

3. Pull end of wire.

4. Compress crimp bead with flat-nose pliers.

5. Finish off by cutting excess wire with wire-cutters. (Attach adjustable chain closures in the same way.)

Attaching a bead tip

1. String a bead tip, then a crimp bead on end of nylon thread.

2. Compress crimp bead with flat-nose pliers. Make sure there are no gaps in the thread.

3. Cut thread 1-2mm away from crimp bead.

4. Enclose crimp bead in bead tip. Close bead tip with flat-nose pliers.

5. Leave a 1-mm space between the bead tip and the last bead strung.

Joining the halves of a perforated finding

1. Cut tabs on bottom half of finding in half to prevent damage to beads and/or nylon thread.

2. Bend tabs down with flat-nose pliers. Bend adjacent tabs first.

3. Slide top of finding into bottom so that tabs fit into slots.

4. Bend down remaining tabs. Place tissue paper between top and bottom half to prevent damage to thread or beads.

5. Finding with two halves joined

HEADPINS AND EYEPINS

Headpins are t-shaped, with a horizontal bar at one end. Eyepins have one rounded end. These pins are often inserted into beads to make separate components.

Rounding ends of pins

1. Insert pin into beads. Cut pin 7-8mm away from end with wire-cutters.

2. Bend shaft of pin at a right angle from base of bead.

3. Bend shaft back into a circle with round-nose pliers.

4. End of pin should lie at bottom of bead, as shown in photo above.

5. These examples show what happens when you don't bend the shaft enough, or bend it incorrectly.

Joining headpins or eyepins

1. Open the rounded end (moving from back to front, not sideways) with flat-nose pliers.

2. Attach component.

3. Close circle with flat-nose pliers.

4. Correctly joined components

JUMP RINGS

These are attached to motifs to connect them to necklaces, and to the ends of necklaces to accommodate clasps.

Opening and closing jump rings

1. Grasp sides of jump ring with flat-nose pliers, and open them by twisting one side toward you and the other away from you.

2. To close a jump ring, follow the opening procedure in reverse. If you twist left and right sides the same amount, you should get good results.

SIDE-CLAMP BEAD TIPS

These are used to join ball chain and clasps.

Attaching a side-clamp bead tip to ball chain

1. Open bead tip and insert ball on end of chain into it.

2. Close bead tip gently with your fingers, then grasp it firmly with flat-nose pliers.

3. Closed bead tip

USEFUL TOOLS

Findings
1. Small jump rings (3-3.5mm diameter)
2. Medium jump rings (4mm diameter)
3. Large jump rings (6mm diameter)
4. Side-clamp bead tip
5. Bead tip
6. Cord tip: Used to enclose ends of leather and other types of cord
7. Crimp beads: For the jewelry in this book, we used medium-sized crimp beads (2mm diameter).

More findings
1. Eyepins: For the jewelry in this book, we use eyepins that are 0.5-0.6mm thick.
2. Headpins: For the jewelry in this book, we use headpins that are 0.5-0.6mm thick.
3. Ear wires
4. Perforated findings: These are available with and without bar pins attached.
5. Clasp
6. Bead caps
7. Spring clasp
8. Adjustable chain closure

Stringing materials
1. Nylon thread: For the jewelry in this book, we used Size 1.5 (0.205mm diameter) transparent thread.
2. Nylon-coated wire: For the jewelry in this book, we used wire measuring 0.24-0.36mm in diameter.
3. Artistic Wire: We used wire measuring 0.4-0.6mm in diameter.
4. Silk thread

Miscellaneous tools
1. Ring stick: Used to measure ring sizes
2. Beading tray: Has a suede lining to keep beads from rolling around
3. Triangular tray: Used to pick up beads from a beading tray

Pliers and cutters
1. **Wire-cutters:** Used to cut pins and wire.
2. **Needle-nose pliers**
3. **Round-nose pliers:** Used to round the ends of headpins and eyepins
4. **Flat-nose pliers:** Used to compress crimp beads
5. **Long-nose pliers:** Used to open jump rings

A selection of Bead work books from J.P.T.

BEAD FANTASIES :
Beautiful, Easy-to-Make Jewelry
by Takako Samejima

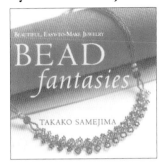

Color photographs of 10 of the 71 pieces include necklaces, bracelets, rings, earrings, brooches, hair ornaments, cell phone straps and eyeglass chains.
66 pages are devoted to brief instructions for the jewelry, supplemented by small color photographs and detailed color drawings. On the last few pages are supplies, and some lessons covering basic bed-stringing, weaving and finishing techniques.
84 pages: 7 1/8×7 1/8 in., paperback US$18.00
ISBN 10: 4-88996-128-3   ISBN 13: 978-4-88996-128-7

BEAD FANTASIES II :
More Beautiful, Easy-to-Make Jewelry
by Takako Samejima

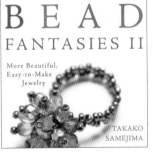

With beautiful color photos, detailed drawings and step-by-step instructions, renowned jewelry designer Takako Samejima makes it easy for even the beginner to create eye-catching, original bead accessories. Bead Fantasies II is divided into three sections. The first part focuses on different accessories designed around one motif, for example a clover, a Diamond-shaped flower, a crown. The second section offers patterns that allow readers to use their own beads to create completely original pieces. The third part, entitled "Bead Items" is organized by type of accessory-rings, earrings, bracelets, necklaces and brooches.
84 pages: 7 1/8×7 1/8 in, paperback US$18.00
ISBN 10: 4-88996-188-7   ISBN 13: 978-4-88996-188-1

BEAD FLOWERS
by Minako Shimonagase

Learn to make exquisite flower creations using simple beads With easy-to-follow instructions and colorful drawings and pictures, Bread Flowers guides readers through the basics, then goes on to offer instructions for creating festive arrangements for special events and occasions, including wedding bouquets, fruits and vegetables for Halloween decorations, Christmas trees and seasonal wreaths.
96 pp., 8 1/4×10 1/4 in., 71 pp. color, 25 b/w pages, paperback US$17.95
ISBN 10: 4-88996-190-9   ISBN 13: 978-4-88996-190-4

ANTIQUE STYLE BEAD ACCESSORIES
by matsuko Sawanobori

Includes both classic and contemporary fashions while providing detailed instructions for making rings, necklaces, chokers, pins, hair ornaments, amulet bags and more.
72 pages: 7 1/2×8 1/2 in., 56 color pages, 16 illustrations, paperback US$15.95
ISBN 10: 4-88996-089-9   ISBN 13: 978-4-88996-089-1

BEADER'S PALETTE

With examples of designs both daring and refined, This book shows how beads of standard sizes and shapes can be combined in dramatic way. With detailed drawings, complete introductions and material guide, it's the perfect guide to learning to make dozens of wearable accessories.
96 pages: 8 1/4×10 1/8 in., 46 full color pages, 32 illlstations, .paperback US$19.00
ISBN 10: 4-88996-097-X   ISBN 13: 978-4-88996-097-6

SAMEJIMA Takako
Jewelry designer

Born in Tokyo in 1970, Ms. Samejima has been fascinated by beads since her elementary school days. Her introduction to beads was through craft books, but she is largely self-taught. Ms. Samejima had been creating bead jewelry for many years in her spare time, but the demand for her work became so great that she opened a studio (Crystalloid) in 1995. Since then, she has been a full-time jewelry designer. Her sophisticated pieces, with their masterful use of color, have been featured in many fashion magazines. She is also the author of My Beaded Accessories, Sweet Bead Collection, Pure Beads and Bead Box, all issued by Nihon Bungeisha. English translations of Bead Fantasies 1 and 2 have increased her already wide audience.